Hoʻonaka

When the Plant Quivers
Legends of Hawaiian Healing Plants

Outskirts Press, Inc.
http://www.outskirtspress.com

ISBN: 978-1-9772-1193-4

Cover and Interior Photos by: Dr. Elithe Manuhaʻaipo Aguiar Kahn. All rights reserved - used with permission.

1. Hoʻonaka "When the Plant Quivers: Legends of Hawaiian Healing Plants / by Dr. Elithe Manuhaʻaipo Aguiar Kahn

Includes bibliographical references and glossary.
2. Ethnobotany Hawaiʻi
3. Legends of Hawaiʻi
4. Medicinal Plants,
5. Hawaiian Folklore
6. Traditional Medicine, Hawaiʻi

Outskirts Press and the "OP" logo are trademarks belonging to Outskirts Press, Inc.

PRINTED IN THE UNITED STATES OF AMERICA

HĀ Breathe!
The Voice of the Shell Sounds, ʻOu Ka Leo O ka Pū

Legends of Hawaiʻi
Lani Goose, Hawaiian Storyteller

Hoʻolei
Activating Makaloa, "The Third Eye"

Aloha
Folk Harp Music Book

If Feet Could Talk
Lomi Wāwae, The Healing Art of Hawaiian Foot Therapy

MU
Descendants
Living Aloha, Living Love, Origins of Hawaiian Sprituality, Remnants of Lemuria

Lilia lanalana, Spider Lily, Crinum Asiaticum

Castor Bean, Palm of Christ, Palma Christi *Ricinus Communis*

CAUTION: Plants can be both beneficial and dangerous. Castor plant seeds are highly poisonous; yet its leaves when patted on the forehead helps to reduce the effects of a raging fever. Its oil moisturizes the skin and thickens the hair. Never use the plants, herbs, or minerals described in this pictorial document for experimentation or medicinal use without first consulting your doctor and a certified Kahuna Lāʻau lapaʻau, herbalist.

The results of all irresponsible applications will be the personal Kuleana, responsibility, of the practitioner and participant. The ideas, procedures, and suggestions in this book are not intended as a substitute for consulting with your doctor or health practitioner. Neither the author nor the publisher shall be held liable for any loss, injury, or damage allegedly arising from any information or suggestion in this book.

Lilikoi, Passionfruit, *Passiflora edulis*

This book is dedicated to the revival of kanaka maoli, native Hawaiian, oral traditions that acknowledge legends as an invaluable source of historical and social information. The goal of this book is to perpetuate the knowledge of healing plants in Hawaiʻi nei. It is written with the great hope that Kamaliʻi, the children, of future generations will carry the torch and continue this tradition.

Acknowledgement
Mahalo Nui

Koki'o, *Hibiscus*

Aloha dear friends, family, and plant lovers. I would like to sincerely thank everyone for their manawale'a, generosity, and mana'o, invaluable knowledge. Without you, this book would not have passed the budding stage much less bloom. There is a saying, "Everyone is entitled to 15 minutes of fame under the sun." This is your time to shine. The rest of the world needs to know how wonderful you all really are.

Special Thanks (Mahalo): To my au Makua mauloa, Eternal Parent; Tim Johns, former CEO, of the Bishop Museum; Ron Cox, former press director, of the Bishop Museum and his wonderful staff for helping to bring this book to life; David Orr, coordinator, of Waimea Valley Audubon Center for his tremendous knowledge and support and most of all for giving this author the thrill of a lifetime by introducing her to an ʻIliahi, a sandalwood tree growing in the wild; Josephine Hoe, the collections manager, who took the time out of her busy day to locate and identify the elusive ʻŌlena, Turmeric, plant; Nathan Wong, Carlton Luka, and Joyce Spores of Foster Gardens for their marvelous networking abilities in finding rare plant specimens; Elizabeth Huppman, horticulturist, at the Lyons Arboretum for her vast knowledge of "who's who" in the botanical arena and the generosity to share it; Noel Kawachi, Waialua High School agriculture consultant, who practices the true meaning of "Aloha" by sharing his knowledge openly and freely giving his plants away to all who promise to give them a good home; Walterbea Aldeguer of the ʻOhana Olamanu Estates Na Kahu of Kaneaʻupu Heiau out in Waianae; To Chelsea Moore of Volcano Village for directions that led me to a Pohā and Laukahi patch.

A special thanks to: Volcano its little Hawaiian herb garden that yielded the mountain Naupaka Kuahiwi plant; Malcolm Nāea Chun for describing and revealing where the Kūkaenēnē plant could be found; and to Sean C. Callahan, horticulturist, at the Hawaiʻi Tropical Botanical Garden on the island of Hawaiʻi for showing and allowing us to shoot a marvelous picture of the ʻAwapuhi Kuahiwi, Soap Ginger, plant after business hours. A special mahalo piha to Aunty Momi Ruane and Kahu Tutu Haddie Kamanu who graciously shared their soul grounding and retrieving prayer.

Family (ʻOhana): Thank you to Gary Kahn, my dear husband. Without his help, encouragement, and computer knowledge this project would have never gotten off the PC; my siblings Wendalen Gonzalez, Sylvia Bertelmann, and Leroy Aguiar for their never-ending support; to Joni Waiolani Owens, my Hānai daughter for providing fresh editing eyes; Aunt Dina Chuensanguansat and Uncle Gwee for their expansive plant knowledge and their huge network of knowledgeable plant enthusiasts; Uncle Billy Pung for helping to find a patch of ʻAlaʻalawainui, of all places, on the grounds of the Bishop Museum; my Hoahānau, cousin, Lani Kiesel, for her loving support, friendship, and uncanny ability to "open doors" and make things happen; and most importantly my Grand Aunt, Reverend Josephine Kiesel whose spiritual guidance, counseling, protection, and healing remedies has safeguarded our ʻOhana throughout the years.

Friends (Hoaloha): Mahalo nui to Duncan Kaʻohu o kaʻala Seto for driving us all over the island of Hawaiʻi in search of plants worth their weight in gold; and Kealohapauʻole (Roz) Manaku for gracing this book with her photographic wizardry and for inspiring and giving me the courage to do the same.

Awapuhi, Yellow Ginger, Zingiber

Ua lehulehu ona mano i ka 'ike o Kanaka Maoli.
Great and numerous is the knowledge of Hawaiian people.

When the Plant Quivers
I ka wa ho'onaka e lā'au

There is Ho'okalakupua, magic, in gathering herbs. *You do not pick the plant; the plant picks you.*

It is a well-known fact among Kahuna Lā'au lapa'au, master herbalists, and Kauka, barefoot doctors, that healing plants possess a subtle vibrating frequency that interacts with the deserving healer. I ka wa ho'onaka e Lā'au, when the plant quivers, its color intensifies and radiates a subtle vibration that draws the attention of the healer to its location. This symbiotic sensitivity is acquired by roaming the forests over the years and communicating with plants.

To become a Kahuna Lā'au lapa'au, specific healing nuances were mandatory to learn. It was paramount to remember the times of the day when various herbs were to be gathered. Herbs used internally were plucked at dawn and those used for external use were plucked at sunset. To pick herbs with unconscious intent produced lack-luster and often negative results.

Using the proper hand in gathering herbs was also strictly observed.

The left hand, the receiving hand, is the favored hand to pick herbs although there are a few exceptions to this rule. The reason remains hūnā, a secret, reserved for Kahuna Lāʻau lapaʻau. As was the custom and still now, students learn by quietly observing. Unfortunately, this native practice often caused gaps in the "Why" of things. Kauka and Kahuna Lāʻau lapaʻau alike adhere to ancient traditions basing their teachings on observation, physical application, and mental communication. All other questions were left for the distracted student to personally solve. The common practice of silently contemplating and mentally asking Au Makua mauloa, the Eternal Parent, "why" proved most resourceful.

How to properly prepare the herbs required years, if not a lifetime, of training. When to prepare the herb was also vital to insure its effectiveness. Healing applications also required specific knowledge; whether to place a leaf face up or face down could very well determine the success of the healing process.

A Kahuna Lāʻau lapaʻau and Kauka learned how to respectfully address a plant as if it were a person. According to tradition, mentioning the name of the sick individual and telling the plant how it could be a great help in healing that person was most important. Thanking the plant for its sacrifice so that another might live would be fulfilling its divine symbiotic purpose here on earth. All of this, of course, would only happen if the plant were willing. The healer would then ask permission to gather up the herb. When, and only when the plant Hoʻonaka, quivered, its consent to share its life force would a Kauka pick the herb. If there was no response, the herbalist moved on. Intuitive healers know that each individual plant is destined for a specific person or animal and would be of little or no use to anyone or anything else. To pick an herb with wild irresponsible abandonment is a travesty and totally unacceptable.

Four Basic Principles of Legend Composition

To help herbal enthusiasts and students remember the healing properties of each plant, barefoot doctors, and Kahuna Lāʻau lapaʻau would weave the most fascinating stories about the healing properties of each plant and where to find them. Here is a formula adhering to four basic principles used by traditional storytellers to orally record history.

1. Always plant seeds of truth
2. Season it with history
3. Garnish it with cultural norms
4. Fire it up with imagination

Each legend within these pages were constructed based on these norms.

Hidden Mystical Construct and Concepts

While plants and herbs are the apparent stars of this book, it would be a travesty not to address the mysticism of the Hawaiian culture that freely flows throughout this pictorial presentation. This is in reference to the mystical construct of the number four. It is most evident in the composition and the forming of these legends. Notice there are four steps to form a story. There were always four meaningful layers within a story. In this way, all listeners, in this case readers, would have an enjoyable measure of understanding according to their breath of cultural knowledge.

Whenever a number four concept is presented, the observer (in this case the reader) is advised to astutely look for the four cultural layers hidden within the story. This four-level concept was once common knowledge and a regular practice among Kanaka Maoli, Native Hawaiians. It went under-ground with the coming of the foreign interventions and ideas. It was a very clever, devious, and convenient way to express frowned upon native traditions right under their ultra conservative noses. The second cultural layer (the realm of the kumu hula, dance instructor) was especially cherished by the general masses where sensual and sexual innuendos were often implied. Natives "in the know" referred to this as Kaona. For a better grasp of the second level, the curious should study the songs ʻOʻopu nui and Maunaloa. As for those that are totally unfamiliar with the fact that there are four layers (not to be confused with meanings) to our native language, may the following examples be helpful in identifying and understanding these layers within each story.

The Names of the Four Levels:

1. **Makaʻāinana** It is literal and intellectual providing information to the public at large.
2. **Kaona** It is sensual and physical best used and understood by Kumu hula, dance instructors.
3. **Kapu** It is poetic and political; a "High Language" exclusively reserved for Royalty, upper crust, and Kahuna nui, High Priest, class.
4. **Hūnā** The realm of mysticism and spirituality not to be confused with religion. Reserved and understood by native Kiloʻuhane, mystics.

The following are two examples of the four layers of understanding prior to the arrival of Haʻole, foreigners.

Example 1:

Level 1 Māunu ka manu, The bird is molting.
Level 2 The person is aging.
Level 3 Look, their hidden truth is being revealed.
Level 4 The person is undergoing a spiritual transformation.

The second example is for the benefit of Haumana Iʻo, spiritual students. It is intended to educate and also provide a tiny glimpse into ancient Kanaka Maoli spiritualism. Little is known, much less in print. For the eager herbalist and spiritually uninterested, skip the second example. Look for the red highlighted Hawaiian phrase and continue from there.

Example 2:

My Eternal Parent (au Makua mauloa)

Level 1:   **Makaʻāinana** (Literal) au Makua mauloa becomes: ʻau Makua mauloa translation: "Deified ancestors"

Level 2:   **Kaona** (Physical and sensual) au Makua mauloa becomes Au… the setting of a net cast forth by the ancestors, to hold us together forever (mauloa) as lovers.

Level 3:   **Kapu** (Poetic, upper crust, royalty, kahuna class) Au Makua mauloa becomes: Au…timeless, eternal; Makua mauloa, Everlasting Parent.

Level 4:   **Hūnā** (Spiritual) Au Makua mauloa (the literal translation gets lost at this level) "Au" identifies the undulating current… streaming forth from the sea of Laʻa Uli Laʻi Laʻi, love and mercy, that deep dark midnight blue space spreading out into the universe. This divine energy is acknowledged as the creative force in the Kumulipo (Hawaiian oral version of creation). This force is Makua… androgynous, genderless Father/Mother combined as one; the "Eternal Parent." A cosmic, everlasting, invisible, spiritual force flowing forth from the cosmic soup (i.e. deep blue space).

The Hawaiian dictionary does not define Au makua with a capital "A." It describes au makua with a small "a" defining a family member, guide, or a god of lesser importance. A word to the neophyte; a small "a" should not be written to address or define the one true GOD. Respectfully use a capital "A" when addressing GOD on paper. Pronouncing a capital "A" verses a small "a" is problematic; it sounds exactly the same when spoken. While it is simple to hear reverence when speaking, it is impossible to hear it when written. The danger here is the loss of respect. Preserving native nuances on paper is a daunting task. Capitalizing the letter "A" when referencing GOD on paper is paramount. The native Hawaiian language is an oral language and its nuances need to be recognized, preserved, and protected whenever possible.

The Hūnā lesson here is to listen, feel, and know (fourth level, intuitive) rather than to think and analyze (first level cerebral, logical). Hūnā falls into the realm of right brain thinking. "I feel, therefore I know," verses left brain cerebral thinking, "I think therefore I am" (René Descartes).

Without its language a nation cannot endure and will surely die.

Presently our native language is enjoying a renaissance. The task to transform our oral language into written form is no doubt a daunting one. To help accomplish this goal, the use of ʻOkina and Kahakō (language markers) has been applied to standardize and to unify the language. This is all well and good for the survival of our culture and the unification of our nation. The major concern and threat are the obscurity and possible loss of the other three layers that are the underlying core support and foundation of our language.

It would be prudent to acknowledge and inform the public there are more layers and depth to the Hawaiian language than what is being written. Information using ʻOkina and Kahakō should be taken literally (first layer/level) as intended.

Aulana ka noʻonoʻo ʻau ana kaʻu ʻolelo!
As ʻŌlelo Kiaʻi, Kalama Cabigon, would say, *"My brain was taking us someplace, but my mouth got lost!"*

Ma hea ʻku nei au? *Now where was I?*

Oh yes, healing plants and herbs!

Each following pictorial and story will provide a *Tonic* and *Conflict* list of herbal uses. It is the most important nuance in the practice of Lāʻau lapaʻau as many herbs will profess to resolve the same ailments. The correct combination of herbs and emotional support is what sets a dabbling herbalist apart from a Kahuna Lāʻau lapaʻau. More often than not, an ailment will require a unique combination of herbs and emotional support to be effective. Barefoot Kauka believe the major underlying source of ailments are based upon unresolved emotional issues. The healing process is twofold. First, resolve the emotional <u>cause</u>, then address the manifested physical <u>effect</u>. Both issues must be recognized and addressed to insure a well-rounded healing solution.

How to Press Herbs, Leaves, and Flowers
There is a good argument for plucking and preserving herbs for prosperity. The back of this book will provide information on several ways to do it.

It is crucial to pule, pray, to protect oneself and ensure success prior to entering the forest or gathering herbs along the coast. Personal cleansing, mentally and physically, prior to picking the herbs had to be strictly observed by the gatherer. To burden the already sick person with one's own negativity and illness was to be avoided at all cost.

Protection Prayer
Pule Māmalu

Wise Kahuna Lā'au lapa'au, herbalists, would recite or chant such a prayer before gathering herbs. To the dilettante seeker, it would be prudent and beneficial to do the same as there are existing ancient kapu, restraints, levied on the land and in the forests of Hawai'i. There are spirits everywhere, so treat the 'aina, land, with loving care.

Tī Leaf, *Cordyline terminalis*

E mai mau Kia'i, E mai ka Pō	Come protector Pō
E nana ia mai, ia mākou	Watch over us
Mai i luna a lalo	From top to bottom
Mai kahi kihi, a ke kahi kihi	From corner to corner
Mai ka Hikina, a ke Komohana	From east to west
Mai ka Uka, a ke Kai	From mountain to the sea
Mai i loko, a ke waho	From inside and out
E mai Kia'i, e mālama ia mākou	Come watch over us.
E pale aku ana, pilikia apau, mai ia mākou	Ward off all trouble from us
Aloha no Kia'i Pō, Aloha no	Love to you protector Pō

Another morsel of esoteric information.

o-u-o-i-a-i-o-u-u-o
Properly arranged
O ou 'oia 'o u uo
This soul of mine chants this prayer loudly.

The theory of "Inside out, outside in" is used to identify and validate ancient chants. Take the last letter from the last word in each line of the chant which are bolded and underlined. The outcome is a sentence that refers to the content of the chant itself. This is a long lost and forgotten style of composition used by the ancients and indicative of the islands of Kanaloa and Kaua'i.

This is a hidden oral code which the Mea oli, chanter, used to inform Ali'i, royalty, and Kahuna Nui, high priests, of the important contents that lay within the chant itself that was reserved for their ears only. This form of chanting is referred to as "Kake, a coded language," and only those educated to its nuances had the ears to hear it. Kake was infused into the chant by quivering or sustaining tones, stops, modulations, and/or repetitions depending on the Mea oli, chanter. This gives a new meaning to the phrase, "Those who have ears, let them hear." It is well known that kanaka maoli culture is deeply seeped in hūnā traditions. Kake is one of them. What is most incredible to this author is how in its written form the rule holds true. "Inside out, outside in" is Kake in written form; the phrase "Mai i Loko a ke waho, from the inside to the outside." The above pule, prayer, refers to the existence of Kake within the oli, chant. This is a clue for Haumana I'o Students of mystic studies, to listen up.

You Do Not Pick The Plant; the Plant Picks You.

The celebrities of this book are a combination of indigenous and Hanai, adopted, botanicals.

Plants will talk if you watch and listen Hidden within these tales and legends are the ancient healing secrets of the plants and herbs of Hawai'i. It is believed the altruistic destiny of healing plants and herbs are to give up their life essence to save others. Kahuna Lā au lapa'au, the barefoot doctors of Hawai'i, would roam the native forests seeking out potential healing plants and herbs by calling out the name of the inflicted and their inflictions. In response, specific healing plants made their presence known by quivering brilliantly in the sunlight catching the eye of the astute healer. All herbalists and barefoot doctors agree, *"You do not pick the plant; the plant picks you!"* In return, Kahuna Lā au lapa'au honored these herbs by orally composing legendary stories that not only preserved their healing capabilities but historical events in which they were the true heroes. These stories of healing plants and herbs is an attempt to acknowledge, perpetuate, and preserve the ancient oral art of recording historical events and healing native traditions in written form.

It is with great hope the next generation will continue the oral tradition of preserving cultural norms through storytelling (Moʻolelo Pōkole).

The personal mystical number for each of the four major demigods of Hawai'i are 1, 4, 5 and 8. These respective individual numbers show their personal association with each plant. An asterisk next to a plant's name recognizes its use in spiritual practices.

Deity	Association
1 Kū	Trees and Stalks
4 Lono	Plants, Nuts, and Fruits
5 Kāne	Kane Seeds, Shrubs, Dirt, Seeds, Shrubs, Dirt, and Vines
8 Kanaloa	Seaweed, Sea Creatures, and Sea Salt

Hawaiian Name	*	Common Name	Deity	Page
'Alaea	*	Red Clay	5	1
'Ala'alawainui		Hawaiian Mint, Poor Man's 'Awa	5	3
'Awamona	*	'Awa, Kava	4	5
'Awapuhi Kuahiwi		Soap Ginger	4	7
Hala, Pūhala		Pandanus, Screwpine	1	9
Hau		Hibiscus, Sea Hibiscus	1	11
Hina hina	*	Dole's Beard, Moss, Air Plant	4	13
'Iliahi	*	Sandalwood	1	15
'Ilima		Prickly Beach Poppy	5	17
'Iwa'iwa		Maidenhair Fern	5	19
Kalo	*	Taro	4	21
Kīnehe		Ghost Needle, Beggar's Tick	5	23
Kō'Uahi a Pele		Red Sugar Cane	1	25
Koali'awa		Morning Glory	5	27

Kuawa		Guava	1	**29**
Kūkaekōlea Pūʻoheʻohe		Job's Tears	5	**31**
Kūkaenēnē		Goose Dung	5	**33**
Kukui	*	Candlenut	1	**35**
Laukahi	*	Plantain	5	**37**
Loli		Sea Slug, Sea Cucumber	8	**39**
Maʻo		Cotton	5	**41**
Maiʻa		Banana	1	**43**
Māmaki		Tea	5	**45**
Naupaka Kahakai		Fan Flower	4	**47**
Nīoi	*	Chile Pepper	5	**49**
Niu	*	Coconut, Tree of Life	1	**51**
Noni Nāmaka o Hina		Noni Apple Eyes of Hina	4	**53**
ʻOhe	*	Bamboo	1	**55**
ʻŌhiʻa ʻai		Mountain Apple	1	**57**
ʻŌlena	*	Ginger, Turmeric	4	**59**
Paʻakai	*	Sea Salt	8	**61**
Pepeiao		Tree Ears, Wood Fungus	5	**63**
Plumeria	*	Frangipani	1	**65**
Pohā		Gooseberry, Musk Tomato, Chinese Lantern	5	**67**
Pōpolo		Black Nightshade	5	**69**
Puakala		Prickly Beach Poppy	5	**71**
Tī Kī Lāʻī	*	Tī Leaf, Good Luck Plant	4	**73**
ʻUala	*	Sweet Potato	5	**75**
ʻUhaloa Hiʻaloa		Marshmallow	4	**77**
ʻUlu	*	Breadfruit, Tree of Plenty	1	**79**

MO'OLELO: LEGEND of 'ALAEA
Red Clay, *Ultisol*

It is said: Kūkona, King of Kaua'i, queried his kāula, prophet, about the outcome of an impending battle. "Victory is yours," his prophet assured. Kūkona abhorred war and like his predecessors preferred to spend time seeking Ho'omālamalama, enlightenment, rather than staining his soul with the blood of a kindred spirit. With a heavy heart, he reluctantly sent his apparent heir Manokalanipō and an army of four hundred men to do battle with the two thousand strong approaching army of Chief Kalaunuiohua.

As predicted, his warriors readily defeated Chief Kalaunuiohua who lived to tell this story. The benevolent Kūkona ordered the defeated chief and his army to be properly fed, clothed, and healed before sending them home laden with gifts and the knowledge of the miraculous healing properties of 'Alaea, red clay.

The red clay remedies relieved pain, regenerated battle-torn skin, boosted the immune system, and shortened the healing process. 'Alaea was also made into a muddy paste and spread over open wounds drawing out the toxic 'ākia that had infected and inflamed the invading forces.

Tipping spears and arrowheads in 'ākia, toxin, was hūnā, a secret, practice of the warriors of Kaua'i. This poisonous plant was kapu, restricted, and not grown on the island itself. It was secretly imported and then prepared for the express purpose of stunning opponents in battle.

But more fascinating were these warriors were spiritually trained to leave their 'I'o, soul essence, in a Tī leaf bundle with a Kahuna Hā'upu'upu, high priest, for safekeeping. This ancient spiritual practice ensured their physical return.

Injuries did occur among the four hundred but none of these injuries were ever fatal. These warriors were often referred to as the Akua, Godly, Warriors of Manokalanipō, which was the original name of Kaua'i Island. The kindness of King Kūkona and fame of his invincible Akua spread throughout Hawai'i and was perhaps another reason why this island was never conquered.

'Alaea: Photo taken at Pūpūkea Ridge.
These pictures were taken while hiking the mountain trail.
Hō'ailona, mystic signs; see the dogs?

ʻALAEA

TONIC
Poison, wounds,
pneumonia, pica,
toxins,
skin regeneration, infections, poison, insect
bites,
parasites, infection,
indigestion,
diuretic,
mineral deficiency,
stomach ailments, pollution.

CONFLICT
Anger, fear, anxiety.

SPIRITUAL USE
Hiʻuwai water
purification ritual.

COMMONALITY
Mineral deficiency,
pollution.

EMOTIONAL LINK
Anger, rage, fear, apprehension,
anxiety.

MO 'OLELO: LEGEND OF 'ALA 'ALAWAINUI
Hawaiian Mint, Poor Man's 'Awa, *Peperomia Tetraphylla*

It is said: Nothing pleasured Kamapua'a, the famous Hog demigod of Hawai'i, more than to graze and then slumber in a mint patch of 'Ala'alawainui. Its sweet pungent aroma not only cleared the nostrils but also allowed Kamapua'a to pleasantly drop into a deep sleep enjoying the placid vivid dreams while allowing his taunt muscles to relax in the process.

In this state of relaxation, his senses were heightened to a point that he could hear the heart-beat of a bird as it fluttered by. And his acute sense of smell could detect fear and hope in the scent of urine being released into the forest air by both man and beast. If it were not for this heightened sense of smell, Kamapua'a would have lost his kinolau, his changeling Hog form body, to the fanatic Maui hunter who relentlessly combed the steep mountain ridges of the Pali in hopes of beheading the demigod to gain favor with the Fire Goddess Pele.

One fateful day, the pungent smell of fresh mint being crushed under the weight of Kamapua'a waft the air and caught the attention of the hunter who was fully aware of all the habits Kamapua'a possessed, especially the habit of sleeping in a patch of mint after he had eaten.

Had it not been for the demigod's heightened sense of smell and light of foot, the head of Kamapua'a would have been delivered as a gift to the Fire Goddess Pele by the Maui hunter.

Accusing the pungent smelling 'Ala'alawainui mint of betrayal, the angry Kamapua'a, in a fit of rage, cursed and peed on the fragrant plant rendering it bitter to the taste and scentless to this day.

'Ala'alawainui: Photo taken at the Bishop Museum. Of all the plants, this one was the most difficult to find. So, cousin Lani called Uncle Billy Pung who remarked, "Go Bishop Museum, get one big patch right outside the building where the Pōhaku stay."

'Ala 'alawainui

TONIC
Phlegm, chills,
congestion,
vagina and anal itch, bladder
and urine infections,
incontinence, swelling,
fever, cancer, tension,
muscle-ache,
sleeplessness,
headache, nerves,
tuberculosis, painkiller,
PMS, dryness, relaxant,
breast stimulant,
sex stimulant.

CONFLICT
Anxious, anger,
indolence, gluttony.

SPIRITUAL USE
Calms the body & mind,
induces mental euphoria,
invokes celestial unification,
meditation.

MOʻOLELO: LEGEND of ʻAWAMONA
ʻAwa, Kava, *Piper methsticum*

It is said: Because of the great famine, Mahoe and his twin sister Mona were orphaned and forced to live with their uncle. To lessen the burden of feeding the two, the uncle arranged to have Mona marry a mean old man. Mona spurned the mean old man's affection and in a jealous rage the old man pierced her heart with an arrow, fatally killing Mona.

With great sorrow, her twin brother Mahoe buried his sister and kept a sleepless watch over her grave for the horrible nightmare of his sister's death haunted his mind. Months passed when a little heart leaf plant sprung up from the grave. Mahoe watched in wonder as it grew, matured, and rooted. Then, the family's aumakua, guardian, ʻIole, the rat, appeared and began to nibble on the plant roots.

As Mahoe watched, the rat went limp and rolled over on its side and fell into a deep, lethargic, peaceful sleep. Instantly, Mahoe knew this to be a Hōʻailona, an omen, so he too chewed on the plant root. It was bitter; it was ʻAwa and numbed his gums but to his amazement it also relaxed him.

For the first time in months, Mahoe fell asleep and was united in dream state with his beloved sister Mona. In his dream, they embraced, laughed, and played throughout the night. At dawn, Mona bid her brother farewell and promised that she would visit him often in his dreams. Upon leaving, Mona told her brother to share the pleasant healing, relaxing wonders of the plant with the villagers so they too could enjoy the peace and joy Mahoe had experienced that night.

"What is the name of this marvelous plant?" a grateful villager asked. Mahoe wistfully smiled and answered, "ʻAwamona," for bitter was his loss and sweet were his dreams of his sister. Today, people call the plant Kava while its original name ʻAwamona has been shortened to ʻAwa.

ʻ**Awamona:** Photo taken in the backyard; notice the heart shaped ʻAwa leaf.

'Awa

TONIC
Tension,
sleeplessness,
fever, PMS,
muscle-ache, headache,
chills, congestion,
dehydration,
painkiller, nerves,
relaxant, joy,
breast stimulant, infection,
sex stimulant,
depression.

CONFLICT
Fear, anxiety,
poverty, self-pity,
sadness.

SPIRITUAL USE
Calms the body and mind
bringing about mental
euphoria,
encouraging
celestial union.

It is said: The high chief Keoua of Kohala Kona had suffered a great loss against Kamehameha and ordered his warriors to retreat. The Fire Goddess Pele intervened on the behalf of Kamehameha slaughtering the remaining forces. Footprints seared into the lava beds at Mauna Iki remain a visual testimony of the massacre. Had it not been for the intervention of the dancing goddess, Laka of the forest, the young boy named Laka Ha'aha'a in her honor would have surely perished that day. Laka Ha'aha'a had been summoned, as was the custom, to become the pae'pae, footstool, for the fleeing Queen of the high chief Keoua. Appearing in a dream, the forest goddess Laka told the boy to stay close to the Queen on the day of the march. On the day of their retreat, the Queen was mysteriously stricken with a massive toothache causing her group to cross the smoldering lava flats last. This delay saved the life of the Queen and her subjects.

But the hero of the day was the boy who cared for the Queen by using the miraculous 'Awapuhi ginger plant. The plant mysteriously sprung up around his feet as he walked the hot lava flats. The sap of this mysterious plant quenched the Queen's thirst and soothed her parched throat. The thick slime it produced coated the inner lining of her lungs saving the Queen from the heat and wrath of Pele. Laka Ha'aha'a also made a poultice for the Queens' toothache and prepared an ointment for her scratches and bruises.

The Queen marveled at this young boy's knowledge which he humbly attributed to Laka, the dancing goddess of the forest. That lucky day, Laka Ha'aha'a realized his most ardent dream. His care for the Queen elevated his position from a lowly footstool to a budding Kumu Hula, dance instructor.

Years later as a young man, Laka Ha'aha'a was summoned to dance before King Kamehameha. He composed a Hula dance telling of the defeat and retreat of Keoua. When asked how he had obtained such detailed information, the young man told the King of his plight as a lowly footstool and quickly added how his aumakua, guardian, Laka, the dancing goddess of the forest, had saved him so that one day he would have the honor of recording the event for the pleasure of the King. The delighted King honored the young man by declaring him the greatest dancing instructor in the district of Kona. And what of the miraculous 'awapuhi ginger plant? Does it still grow on the lava flats? 'A'ole, no, only in the lush tropical forests of the goddess Laka from where it came.

'Awapuhi Kuahiwi: Photo taken at Hawai'i Tropical Botanical Garden on the island of Hawai'i.

'Awapuhi Kuahiwi

TONIC
Toothache, thirst,
headache, cuts,
bruises, sores,
soap, ringworm,
sprains,
stomach issues,
nausea, congestion,
muscle and joint pains, burns,
infection,
circulation, heartburn,
moisturizer.

CONFLICT
Fear,
anger,
apprehension.

MOʻOLELO: LEGEND of HALA, PŪHALA
Pandanus, Screwpine, *Pandanus odoratissimus*

It is said: Nalalaniapilihala, a little girl, was orphaned by a rough tidal wave that destroyed her entire village. The act of fetching water from a fresh water cave high on a mountain ridge saved her life.

Her wails of grief pieced the heart of Pūhala the pandanus tree and guardian of the cave. Pūhala gently drooped its thorny leaves around Nala to comfort her intertwining itself forming a cradle to hold and rock the crying child to sleep. From that day on, they became ʻOhana, family.

Over the years, Nala learned the art of weaving the most beautiful mats from the old Pūhala tree. She spent the better part of her days gathering and preparing the long, green, glossy leaves by first removing its thorns and then drying them. Over the years, Nala lined the entire cave with the most intricate and wondrous designs, a loving tribute to the old Pūhala tree. She also learned of its powers to heal infections, sores, and cuts she accidentally experienced while removing the thorny rib from the leaves and how the dust from its tree trunk nodules eased her asthmatic wheezing chest.

One day, a voyaging canoe landed on the isle in search of water and found the cave, Nala, and the old Pūhala tree. They were awed by the beauty of the mats Nala had created. They pleaded with the young woman, who was orphaned so long ago, to come and live with them and to share her skill of weaving with their village. Sadly, Nala refused to leave Pūhala who had grown old and weak.

Pūhala knew its time of recreation had come and so instructed Nala to leave giving her four magic Pūhala nuts to plant in her new homeland. This act would ensure the spirit of Pūhala would be with her always. Upon arriving in her new homeland, Nala did as Pūhala instructed and planted the magic nuts. They immediately sprouted into four Pūhala trees producing glossy, vibrant leaves with which Nala wove and used to train the women of the village. Through the ages, the most common and popular form of weaving is called Nala, in honor of the maiden of the Pūhala cave.

Hala, Pūhala: Photo taken in downtown Honolulu. Fond memories of outings at Haena and the Waikanaloa wet cave on the island of Kauaʻi. Whenever tourists or family visited, Dad would give them the grand tour. We kids would go along for the ride and listen to Dad tell the most fascinating stories of the area. I must have gotten the gift of gab from him!

Hala
PūHala

TONIC

Chest pains,
heart ailments,
sores,
after-birth tonic,
scratches,
internal spasms,
cleanser, backache, asthma,
skin irritation,
tuberculosis,
urinary tract,
infections,
arthritis,
stomachache,
aphrodisiac,
inflammation.

CONFLICT

Fear, anger, sadness,
death, abandonment.

SPIRITUAL USE

Hoʻokalakupua magic,
implications.

It is said: The birth of Chief Luanuʻu was in peril. Queen Kaea suffered the pangs of a dry birth. Attending the Queen was the famous Pale keiki, midwife, ʻUlu, and three akua spirit sisters from Kahiki.

The solution to the difficult birth eluded all of them. Fearing for mother and child, Melemele, the youngest akua sister, transformed into a brilliant yellow hibiscus instructing ʻUlu, the midwife, to feed the queen the slimy sap that oozed from the nose of the flower bud in hopes of lubricating the birth canal and easing the pain. But much to her dismay, it didn't work. At noon, ʻEhu, the second akua sister, transformed into an orange hibiscus instructing ʻUlu to do the same with hopes of lubricating and strengthening the exhausted Queen but, uwē, uwē, alas, it too did not.

At sunset, Ahi, the oldest and boldest sister, transformed into a red hibiscus; but again, the slimy tonic she produced was sadly not strong enough.

As fate would have it, Hauʻoki, their brother, also witnessed the life and death situation and was compelled to moved his spirit into the trunk of the hibiscus tree that held the floral essences of his three akua sisters. He instructed ʻUlu, the midwife, to strip the bark from the tree and combine its slippery ooze with the yellow, orange, and red hibiscus slime his sisters had produced.

The magical combination of brother and sisters proved to be the perfect solution. The Lāʻau lapaʻau, medicine, immediately relaxed the Queen's constricted organs and relieved the pain associated with birthing. It also permitted the liver and kidneys to cool and settle down allowing for the natural flow of body fluids. Had it not been for the three akua sisters and Hauʻoki, the royal lineage of Wākea might have ended that day. As a testimony to the event, the sea bush with its three shades of flowers was named Hau to honor Hauʻoki and his three akua sisters from Kahiki.

Hau: Photo taken at Waikiki Beach. This legend intertwines healing plants and island history concerning the birth of the son of Chief Luanuʻu.

Hau

TONIC
Laxative,
purgative,
fever, congestion,
inflamed internal
organs,
swollen kidney,
fatty liver,
stiff joints,
infection, thirst,
lubricant,
moisturizer
coolant,
relaxant,
hormone
imbalance.

CONFLICT
Anxiety, fear,

MOʻOLELO: LEGEND of HINA HINA
Dole's Beard, Moss, Air Plant, *Tillandsia usneoides*

It is said: The young teenager began to waste away. The blood circulation to her hands was completely cut off baffling modern medicine. No blood reached her fingertips, yet the rest of her body functioned normally. Her hands ached incessantly causing the teenager to rub her hands to the point of rubbing her fingerprints off. Something toxic was attacking her from within.

"ʻIno hoʻokalakupua, it is sorcery," kahuna pule, the priestess, declared. She then grabbed a hand full of Hina hina moss. She began pounding and mashing it for its poisonous juice carefully preparing it to fight poison with poison. She imbued the concoction with other herbs to be ingested under strict supervision while specific prayers were recited. This daily ritual lasted 40 days.

The gift of ʻIke pāpā lua, second sight, had revealed the teenager had embarrassed a boy by publicly slapping his face. This humility sent his grandmother into a rage. She cursed the young girl commanding the hands that abused her Moʻopuna kane, her grandson, should wither and fall off. Lucky for the young girl, her auntie was a kahuna pule, priestess, and a Lāʻau lapaʻau, herbalist practitioner. It was her aunt who discovered the poisonous plot by means of Wehe ʻike Paipala, Bible prophecy. The Kahuna pule tried to arrange a Hoʻopono pono, conflict and resolution session, but to no avail.

Proper apologies were made but uwē, alas, it was not accepted making it crucial to find and destroy the hidden ʻeke bag containing articles of the girl's hair and bird bones. As her auntie predicted, the ʻeke bag was found buried under the steps of the girl's home and burnt. This action broke the curse freeing the entrapped spirit of the girl, allowing blood to flow freely back into the girl's hands and fingertips again. She lives to tell the tale.

Hina hina: Photo taken deep in Pauoa Valley. This family story is true.

Hina Hina

TONIC
Poison (physical
& spiritual),
absorbent,
heavy metals,
lead, copper,
nickel,
manganese,
toxins, venom.

CONFLICT
Superstition,
pride, anger,
jealousy,
vindictive.

SPIRITUAL USE
Spirit protection,
mending gaping holes
in the Pilikino
(the esoteric body
blue print),
life force,
energizer..

MO 'OLELO: LEGEND of 'ILIAHI
Sandalwood, *Santalum Album*

It is said: Kuna, a shape-shifting lizard man, desired the maiden 'Iliahi for his own not only for her beauty but more importantly her unique knowledge of healing using tropical oils.

'Iliahi was the most celebrated Lomilomi masseuse in all of Hawai'i. Ila, birthmarks, on her left hand acknowledged her healing abilities at the time of her birth. The clearly etched stars in the palm of her hand assured her family of her destiny as a masseuse. Coming from this specific line of healers, 'Iliahi learned the art of rendering and mixing herbs and healing oils that were kapu, held in reserve, by her 'Ohana, family.

Desperate for this invaluable knowledge, Kuna the shape-shifter devised himself a plan. He would disguise himself as an old feeble man with the most crooked spine. In this way, he would surely gain her sympathy. Once they were alone, he would steal her away. His ploy worked!

Out of the crowds waiting to be healed, she signaled the old feeble man to come into her hut. As Kuna undressed, the sight of his gnarled and crooked spine filled 'Iliahi with overwhelming compassion. She reached for a small coconut 'Apu, cup, filled with a special oil she had just rendered from a sandalwood tree.

This aromatic healing oil was made to relax and warm the spine, ease the pain, dislodge the virus, and dissolve the emotional blockage that held the feeble man prisoner. Little did she know of his evil intentions to kidnap her, but uwē, alas, the healing warmth of the oil not only penetrated the skin of the old man but scalded the hidden sensitive lizard skin beneath it.

Kuna the shape-shifter leaped up shrieking trying to rub the oil off his back as he howled in agony. The withering pain caused Kuna to change back into his original Mo'o, lizard, form revealing his true self. 'Iliahi screamed in horror alerting the villagers who hurried to her rescue. In shame, Kuna scampered out of the hut and into the forest cursing the oil for revealing the truth deep down within.

'**Iliahi:** Photo taken at Pūpūkea Ridge. This old remedy of using 'Iliahi oil to warm the spine is indicative of Kaomi lomilomi, a massage technique specific to the island of Kaua'i..

'Iliahi

TONIC
Cancer, tumor, virus,
infections,
cold sores,
acne, wrinkles, scars,
pineal, stimulant,
nerve disorders, electromagnetic,
blockages,
spinal deformities,
immune system.

CONFLICT
Self-scorn, rejection,
bitterness, remorse,
spiritual congestion,
repressed anger, fraud.

SPIRITUAL USE
Activate the aka cord,
cleanse the Pilikino
(esoteric body blueprint),
open the Makaloa
(Third-eye)
& the Piko Manawa
(crown chakra),
activate the pineal gland.

MO'OLELO: LEGEND of 'ILIMA
Prickly Beach Poppy, *Sida fallax*

It is said: Once, the 'Ilima blossom was as white as the clouds above and that the fatty sweat of the demigod Kamapua'a turned it yellow. He was jealous of the love that existed between the Princess Kumuleilani and the young Chieftain Kua'iwa. Once, Kamapua'a had approached wheezing and panting his romantic desires but Kumuleilani denied his advances scoffing at his fat, unconditioned, stubby body; her rejection only made Kamapua'a lust for her all the more.

Each day, he would secretly watch Kumuleilani gather the beautiful, tiny, white, delicate paper blossoms from the shoreline in the early morning just before dawn. It was her daily routine to gather and string a lei, garland, of love for her beloved Kua'iwa, eight hundred flowers to be exact. It was also the time of the morning when Kumuleilani would purify herself discarding her Kihei, garment, to bathe in the ocean. The sight of her body glistening in the early morning light drove Kamapua'a into a sexual frenzy, and as she emerged from the ocean he attacked her.

Her screams alerted Kua'iwa who rushed to her rescue. In a death-roll, Kua'iwa and Kamapua'a tumbled down the shoreline crushing the delicate white blooms in their wake. The yellow, fatty sweat oozed from the pores of Kamapua'a staining the white paper-thin blossoms forever yellow. Though the battle was fierce, it ended quickly. Kua'iwa handedly defeated the short-winded, unconditioned demigod. In shame, Kamapua'a scampered up the craggy shoreline and disappeared into the forest never to roam the shorelines again.

As for Kumuleilani, she continued with glee to gather the now yellow stained 'Ilima blossoms weaving the tiny paper flowers into a lei as a tribute to her Chief's fitness and bravery.

'Ilima: Photo taken in Pāpakolea. Each year, all islands display their unique island color, song, and flower at their May Day floral festivals. The golden regal 'Ilima blossom represents the island of Oahu, the Royal Capital of Hawai'i.

'Ilima

TONIC

Constipation,
vagina issues,
lung congestion,
fever, fatty liver,
vein blockages,
blood purifier,
blood pressure, congestion,
strengthens
immune system.

CONFLICT

Lust, envy, pride,
anger, danger,
rejection,
jealousy,
disapproval,
insecurity.

MO'OLELO: LEGEND of 'IWA'IWA
Maidenhair Fern, *Adiantum capillusveneris-L*

It is said: The lovely maiden 'Iwa'iwa of Honomu had the most luxurious, shiny hair in all of Hawai'i. Indeed, she was beautiful and her long flowing, thick blue-black hair glistened in the sunlight. Her hair was most desired by the lusty old balding Molemole. He was a Kauwā, an outcast, who lived in a cave near 'Akaka Falls.

Mindful were the maidens of the village who ventured into the 'Akaka Falls rainforest for a swim. All knew of the sly, old man and his eccentric ways. His congested cough and wheezing characteristically gave the women a warning of his presence in which case they would quickly return to the village.

They were warned never to go alone, but one dreadful day the maiden of Honomu made a fatal mistake. She decided to go for a swim by herself. The sight of her hair floating on the water like blue seaweed increased the desire of Molemole to abduct the maiden for her hair.

On her way back up the path, 'Iwa'iwa took a shortcut and unknowingly walked by the entrance of his hidden cave. Molemole seized the opportunity grabbing the maiden by her ankles dragging her into his craggy rock cave; as he did, he commanded his cave entrance to slam shut never to open again entombing Molemole and the lovely maiden of Honomu forever.

But uwē, alas, he had commanded the entrance to close too quickly and as it did the long flowing hair of 'Iwa'iwa that trailed behind her was caught outside of the cave entrance robbing Molemole of what he desired most.

The goddess of the forest Lea who witnessed the abduction took pity on the maiden's plight and transformed her hair dangling outside the rocky cave wall into a lacy fern naming it 'Iwa'iwa after the lovely maiden of Honomu.

Today maidenhair fern can still be found dangling from the craggy rock-face walls of the valley that line the pathway to 'Akaka Falls. As for the entrance to the cave of Molemole, it remains a secret to this day.

'Iwa'iwa: Photo taken while hiking the old Nu'uanu Pali mountain trail.

19 🌿 DR. ELITHE MANUHA'AIPO AGUIAR KAHN

Iwa'Iwa

TONIC
Allergy, warts,
fungus,
lung congestion,
fever, asthma,
sore throat,
phlegm, boils, bronchitis,
hepatitis, spasm,
fatty liver,
poison,
gallstones, sores,
mucus, virus,
parasites, colds,
fever, obesity,
flu, hair-loss,
shiny hair rinse.

CONFLICT
Seething anger, envy,
loneliness,
neglect.

MO'OLELO: LEGEND of KALO
Taro, *Colocasia esculenta-L*

It is said: The most sacred and blessed celestial union that could occur on Earth was a union between a Wohi Chief and a sacred daughter. In this way, the royal bloodlines of the demigods were kept pure and so it was with Wākea and his youngest daughter Niaupi'o.

The first child born from this sacred union was E'epa, a gelatinous formless offspring. This child was named Hāloa and because of his gelatinous formless body the child was sent to live among the demigods in the Eastern heavenly realm of Lani kuaka'a. The second child from this sacred union was also named Hāloa in honor of his formless elder brother. This second child is recognized as the human ancestral parent of Hawai'i.

As was the custom, Hāloa the first born was appointed as his younger brother's guardian and guide. There was much concern because this second child took on a physical earthly form. It could not live on air alone like the other demigods. Air passed right through the baby's body. A nourishing substance had to be created or else the child would not survive.

All in heaven were set to task to find a life sustaining food source, but each food presented irritated the poor child's tummy causing the little baby's stomach to painfully swell and release the foulest smelly odor and liquid.

Lumps, warts, and boils erupted all over the poor baby whose little body was desperately fighting to expel the poisons and parasites that each of the strange foods possessed. Thankfully, out of his gelatinous form his older brother Hāloa created the perfect solution. It was a soft, sticky, and gooey substance that clung to the ribs and intestinal walls of the child. It provided the baby with the necessary nourishment the child desperately needed to survive.

Hāloa the formless, called this nourishing food Poi. Hāloa lovingly offered his kinolau, spirit form, as a staple food source for his baby brother. Poi eventually became the staple food "source of life" for all Polynesians, a gift from both brothers to all mankind. To eat Kalo was to spiritually nourish the body from within and out.

Kalo: Photo taken at Moanalua Gardens. Legend is based on the Creation story as told by Martha Beckwith, the garden's historian.

Kalo

TONIC
Loose bowels,
stomach issues,
indigestion,
constipation, gas,
pain, thrush, cysts,
boils, internal
bleeding ulcers,
swelling,
infection,
pink eye,
parasites.

CONFLICT
Anger,
lust, fear,
rejection,
anxiety,
confusion.

SPIRITUAL
Soul sustenance,
physical embodiment of God..

MOʻOLELO: LEGEND OF KĪNEHE
Ghost Needle, Beggar's Tick, *Bidens pilosa*

It is said: In the days when four hundred thousand demigods roamed the Earth, the people were ever alert and weary of strangers who came to their home. Fear and anxiety struck the core of the hearts of each villager.

The common right to be fed, clothed, and sheltered by those who had was understood by all villagers who, without hesitation, complied. But these were the days when both the good and vicious demigods roamed the earth unchecked and caused much confusion and misery.

The exhausting task of trying to determine who was real and not caused depression and fear among the people; for often as a form of punishment, the vicious demigods took their children for slaves.

It was Kahuna Kīnehe who devised a simple plan to detect the troublesome demigods. He ordered the villagers to plant an unassuming Laʻau plant laden with tiny black stickers along the pathway leading to their homes and near the entrance to their huts.

When ordinary people approached their home, the stickers would cling to their clothing and body hair identifying them as human. But when a demigod walked by, the sticky needles of the plant fell to the wayside for nothing could cling to a ghost body form.

This simple detection allowed the villagers to be extra mindful and respectful of these changeling demigods in hopes of avoiding their wrath. Grateful old timers still call the Koʻokoʻolau plant, Kīnehe in honor of the Kahuna who devised the demigod and ghost detection scheme.

Kīnehe: Photo taken at Hoʻomaluhia Botanical Park. Legend in loving memory of Princess Ruth.

Ko'oko'olau
Kīnehe

TONIC
Blood purifier,
poison, infection,
purgative,
tension, tumors,
poor circulation,
fatty liver,
mucous, flu, colds,
stress, stimulant,
blood disorder,
fatigue,
skin toner.

CONFLICT
Depression,
fear,
anxiety,
anger,
frustration.

MO'OLELO: LEGEND of KŌ 'UAHI A PELE
Red Sugar Cane, *Saccharum officinarum rubrum*

It is said: Kamapua'a, the Hog demigod, had an ugly stature. His skin was rough and tough as leather; his body hair resembled that of a pig, thick and hard as boar bristles. Yet, he was the undisputed, most romantic suitor in Hawai'i. To be bedded by Kamapua'a was considered highly prestigious among ambitious women seeking to obtain a higher social status among the villagers.

Kamapua'a went through great measures to lure and bed not only the village maidens but also the goddesses of old Hawai'i. His most famous conquests were the sisters of the Fire Goddess Pele. This infuriated Pele as Kamapua'a was betrothed to her. Not by choice but mandated by the Gods.

Kamapua'a deemed himself quite the lover with a little help from Makanikeoe his personal Kahuna Aloha, his crafty love potion brew master. Once under the potion's spell, women were helplessly defenseless and submitted themselves to the lusty Hog demigod.

Makanikeoe provided Kamapua'a with a love tonic consisting of eight different herbs: 'Awa, Nīoi, 'Iwa'iwa, Puakala, 'Ala'alawainui, and two prized secret ingredients known only by members of the Kahuna Aloha Class. The remaining two ingredients that regulated its potency and intensity still remain a closely guarded secret today. The final ingredient was a heavily laced sweetener, Kō'Uahi a Pele, a red variety of sugar cane specifically used for love potions. The sweet potion mixed well with food made it totally undetectable.

The unsuspecting victims often talked about the fragment scent of fern just before a mild sense of euphoria and temporary amnesia set in. The entire unwanted encounter rendered them helpless. The irony is the dastardly vulgar deed was committed by Kamapua'a, the demigod PIG.

Kō'Uahi a Pele: Photo taken at Waimea Botanical Garden. The Legend was inspired by Kame'eleihiwa Lilikala whose stories on Kamapua'a are most entertaining.

Kō
Uahi a Pele

TONIC

Skin, cuts, acne,
scars, infections,
hiccups, nausea,
wounds, toxins,
sex stimulant,
fever,
boosts appetite
and immune
system,
energizer,
aids liver,
weight loss,
body organs,
kidneys, diabetes,
bad breath, gums,
brittle bones,
fingernails, cancer,
mineral shortage.

CONFLICT

Rejection, lust,
bitterness, anger,
fear, jealousy,
self-pity.
These are healing benefits of
Sugarcane Juice,
NOT refined sugar crystals.

MO'OLELO: LEGEND of KOALI'AWA
Morning Glory, *Ipomoea congesta*

It is said: Kaha'i and Wai'olani were lovers since childhood and spent much of their youth at Kāpuhi beach on the isle of Moloka'i. What should have been a long, happy, and peaceful life together was abruptly shortened by King Kalunui'ohua of Hawai'i who conquered the island of Maui and now was advancing on to Moloka'i.

Kaha'i was called to arms as were all the young men from the village. Though they fought bravely, the men of Moloka'i were no match for the fierce warriors of Kalunui'ohua. Wai'olani found Kaha'i severely wounded laying helpless with his arms and legs broken and left for dead.

Wai'olani quickly gathered the roots of the Koali'awa, the Morning Glory, vine that sprawled along the beach. She quickly pounded it into a poultice using the mashed remedy to pack his wound and dress his injury. She used the vines to help set and bound his broken bones. She also made a bitter tea to help heal him internally, but uwē, alas, a search party of warriors found them.

Wai'olani threw herself over Kaha'i but to no avail. A heartless warrior drove his Ihe, spear, through her back piercing her heart and the heart of Kaha'i who lay helpless under her. Their blood mingled in death and seeped into the sand.

Their love and devotion to each other touched and inspired Kanaloa, the demigod of life and death. "Let not their true love be forgotten," Kanaloa declared and commanded the Morning Glory plant to bloom forth two flowers on the same vine: a blue flower in memory of Kaha'i and the pink blossom for Wai'olani.

To this day, the early morning light beckons the spirit of Kaha'i which appears as a blue flower, and at this stage, the vine is most potent and used for external injuries. As the day progresses, the flower turns to a delicate pink hue allowing the gentle spirit of Wai'olani to impregnate the blossom with a subtle healing energy for internal use. Forever entwined, the spirits of the two lovers will perpetually live on in the Koali'awa vine.

Koali'awa: Photo taken on the "Big Island." The legend was inspired by Likeke R. McBride, historical account of King Kalaunuiohua battles.

Koali'awa

TONIC
Purifier,
broken bones,
injured tendons,
stress,
relaxant,
purifier,
torn tendons,
cartilage and
muscle,
back pain,
physical stress,
wound dressing,
tea tonic,
purgative.

CONFLICT
Violence,
fear,
anger.

MOʻOLELO: LEGEND OF KUAWA
Guava, *Psidium guajava*

It is said: Puaʻa, the Pig, had eaten too much ʻInamona, Kukui nut relish, the night before. So now, he was in desperate need of finding something to stop him from purging and pooping so much. While walking along a mountain trail, Puaʻa noticed Moa, the rooster, perched on a branch of a Kuawa tree and asked the rooster if it knew of a cure for his problem. Moa crowed, "Try the tender leaves from this tree."

"Would you be so kind as to pluck me a few?" Puaʻa helplessly groaned. "Indeed," the rooster clucked in sympathy and plucked a few fresh young leaf buds from the tree dropping them down to the Pig waiting below. Puaʻa quickly chomped them down and much to his delight it worked!

Not only did it stop him from pooping, but it also settled his upset stomach and soothed his inflamed ulcer. He also noticed that it left his "boar breath" fresh and sweet for a change. And it actually relieved the lesions in his mouth from rooting and grubbing for ʻuala, sweet potatoes and kukui nut shells.

"This is Maikaʻi no, wonderful! How can I repay you?" Puaʻa squealed with delight. "Perhaps another day," Moa crowed and flew away.

Later that afternoon when crossing a mountain stream, the pig came upon a pack of wild dogs that had cornered Moa the rooster. Moa was caught off guard while taking a bird bath. Unable to fly way, Moa hid behind some rocks.

Just as the dogs clawed away, the last rock protecting the rooster, Puaʻa, the pig, charged the pack of dogs. Fur went flying all over the place. It ended with howling dogs yelping and running off into the forest and Puaʻa, the pig, saving the day.

"Mahalo nui, Thank you so much," the rooster crowed. "It's Meaʻole, no big thing," the pig snorted. "One good deed deserves another," Puaʻa said as he trotted away.

Kuawa: Photo taken in Pauoa Valley. This legend was created while sitting under a guava tree on the banks of Nuʻuanu stream.

Kuawa

TONIC
Indigestion, loose
bowels, ulcers,
internal bleeding,
bad breath,
cold sores,
stomachache,
infection, cramps,
sprains,
cuts and boils,
skin toner.

CONFLICT
Anxiety,
fear of poverty,
fear of hunger,
gluttony.

MO'OLELO: LEGEND OF KŪKAEKŌLEA, PŪʻOHEʻOHE
Job's Tears, *coix lacryma jobi*

A Famous Urban Legend of the Birth of Kamehameha the Great

It is said: Kekuiʻapoiwa, the mother of King Kamehameha, was prone to pica cravings. Her abnormal craving for red clay, red fish, or anything red was the reason why Kekuiʻapoiwa insisted on eating a red eyeball of a chief. This was an unacceptable craving even by Kahuna nui, High Priest, standards.

It has long been known by Kahuna Laʻau lapaʻau, herbalists, baby ailments were predetermined by what was going on between the mother and child during pregnancy. Both positive and negative emotions of the mother were passed onto the child. If left unchecked, these negative craving emotions of the queen would eventually manifest as physical ailments for the child. The consensus was, if left unfulfilled, the baby would suffer such evidence in the form of drooling most unbefitting for a chief! This, of course, was unacceptable. So as a befitting substitute, the craving Queen was given a red eyeball of a man-eating shark. This shark was a kinolau, changeling form, of Lehuaokalani, the Red Shark goddess of the sea.

The red shark eyeball was rolled in a powder of crushed Kūkaekōlea Pūʻoheʻohe seeds. It was this powder that nourished the Queen and stopped her Pica cravings, not the shark eyeball. But as fortune would have it, this act of eating the eyeball aligned the future King Kamehameha with the Red Shark goddess of the sea giving him "Ike Pāpālua, second sight," ESP, and psychic abilities.

Another twist of fate was a Shark-fin shaped birthing stone, a kinolau, changeling land form, of Lehuaokalani. The Queen had once visited the birthing stone, and by happenstance she aligned herself and her unborn child with the land image of the Red Shark goddess as well. Queen Kekuiʻapoiwa fortuitously secured her son's prowess on both land and sea. The dual prowess of the Red Shark goddess Lehuaokalani would give the child a shark's formidable stature, aggressive nature, and a robust immune system. These were all incredible characteristics that would be imprinted onto the child at the time of birth. This would be an Aliʻi, a Royalty, born with immense mana, supernatural powers. This historical phenomenon proved itself to be true. Kamehameha was the first and only King to unite the Hawaiian Isles under a single rule.

Kūkaekōlea, Pūʻoheʻohe: This Photo was taken at Hoʻomaluhia Botanical Garden. The Shark-fin stone, Lehuaokalani, is presently hidden at Kūkaniloko among the birthing and healing stones of Wahiawa on the island of Oahu.

KūKaeKōlea, Pūʻoheʻohe

TONIC
Cravings, swelling,
lung congestion,
loose bowels,
pus eliminator,
skin irritations,
dank lungs,
tuberculosis,
mucus, infection,
sterilizer,
blood purifier,
dehydrator,
headache,
fatty liver,
fever, ulcers,
joint pain,
gum infection,
chest congestion,
urinary tract issues.

CONFLICT
Lust,
greed,
envy,
gluttony.

MOʻOLELO: LEGEND of KŪKAENĒNĒ
Goose Dung Berries, *Coprosma emodeoides*

It is said: The trail was difficult for Aiwohikupua to get to the summit of Mauna Kea. It took the handsome lover of Poliʻahu, the snow queen, five days to reach the top of the mountain from the shoreline of Hilo Bay. And what made the trek most difficult, Aiwohikupua had to cross the rugged lava fields of the Fire Goddess Pele, the sister and rival of Poliʻahu.

Pele was smitten with the handsome warrior with ʻeleʻele, dark and warm, eyes. Pele continuously tried to seduce and steal him away from her sister. Whenever the handsome warrior from Kauaʻi came to visit, Pele's pet nēnē, geese, would alert her. But unknown to the Fire Goddess, her sister the snow queen would disguise herself as a nēnē, goose, and joined the flock of birds who flew down the coastline to greet and accompany Aiwohikupua as he made the long and difficult journey to the top of Mauna Kea.

To gain their loyalty and keep her disguise a secret, Poliʻahu gifted the geese with a shrub laden with succulent blackberries. In this way, she could see if her lover remained true to her. How thrilled she was to see her lover reject Pele and her advances. Each time Pele failed, Poliʻahu, in her kinolau, changeling form, as a nēnē, goose, would secrete a little blackberry to mark the spot. It wasn't long before the mountain slopes were heavily dotted with blackberry shrubs.

One day, Pele noticed that her pet nēnē, geese, were eating these shiny blackberries with great relish and wondered where it came from. Curious, she tried a mouthful and much to her dismay she experienced a bowel movement that lasted for three days.

"That is what you get for trying to seduce Aiwohikupua," her sister Poliʻahu taunted. Pele tried to deny the fact, but the clever snow queen pointed to each spot marked by a shrub where Pele tried and failed to steal the heart of the warrior. "Uwē you Kūkaenēnē, alas you bird dung spy," Pele hissed trying to insult her sister. Poliʻahu laughed, "A perfect name for the plant that purged you for your misdeeds, Kūkaenēnē indeed," the snow queen laughed and flew away.

Kūkaenēnē: Photo taken at Hawaiʻi Volcanoes National Park. Finding this plant was like taking a step back in time. Lani and I were desperate; the sun was setting, and we were about to give up when we bumped into Malcolm Nāea Chun, the modern-day guru of laʻau lapaʻau plants. He just happened to be hiking along the rim of Kilauea Volcano that day. He nonchalantly directed us to its precise location along Desolation Trail. As always, au Makua mauloa provided us with the perfect Kupuna (elder). In God We Trust!

Kūkaenēnē

TONIC
Bowel blockage,
cuts, bruises,
boils, purgative,
blood purifier,
clothing dye,
rich in nitrates,
source of protein,
enzymes and amino acids.

CONFLICT
Envy,
anger,
pride,
lust.

MO'OLELO: LEGEND of KUKUI
Candlenut, *Aleurites moluccana*

It is said: Kamapua'a, the changeling Hog demigod, had many kinolau, changeling forms; an invisible fleeting spirit, a fragrant fern, and the Kukui nut tree were among his favorite disguises.

His choice pastime was to spy and watch the women of the village bathe in the cool mountain streams of Hawai'i. This is why there are so many Kukui nut trees that grow along the banks of mountain streams.

Though aware of his kolohe, naughty mischievous ways, the village maidens were helpless and frustrated never sure of the demigod's presence as his invisible life-force could move swiftly from leaf to leaf, tree to tree, and up and down the valley. However, the Fire Goddess Pele, being a demigod as well, easily detected her mischievous betroth and flushed him out of hiding.

Taking pity on the village maidens, Pele taught them how to detect the presence of Kamapua'a before bathing by closely looking at the leaves of the Kukui nut trees.

Pele warned, "Should the Kukui nut tree bare five-pronged leaves that resembled a boar's head, ears, and tusks, do not bathe there because Kamapua'a was surely watching." Pele went on to say, "Bathe only in the presence of a three-pronged leafed Kukui nut tree where the leaves resembled a pig's foot in flight." This would mean his back was facing away from the bathing pool indicating the Fire Goddess Pele was hot on his heels and that Kamapua'a was fleeing for his life!

Kukui: Photo Photo taken in Pauoa Valley. Legend inspired by a Kukui tree in the backyard with its branches suspended over Nu'uanu stream.

Kukui

TONIC
Thrush,
mouth and
cold sores,
sunburn,
chapped lips,
purifier,
lazy bowels,
high blood pressure,
ulcers,
chest and lung congestion,
infection,
skin lesions,
toothache,
bad breath,
moisturizer.

CONFLICT
Lust, gluttony,
envy, anxiety,
repressed anger,
frustration.

MOʻOLELO: LEGEND of LAUKAHI
Plantain, *Plantango major*

It is said: Once again the mad hunter from Maui had routed Kamapuaʻa, the hog demigod, and had chased him for many days and nights following his tracks along the Koʻolau mountain range. The hunter trekked through brushes, brambles, mud, and streams searching every valley and marshland leaving no hog hole unchecked. Kamapuaʻa was exhausted by the relentless chase.

Kamapuaʻa was forever invading Pele's domain leaving his hoofprints and dung along the leeward trails irritating the Fire Goddess. His amorous lovemaking among the common women of the lowlands was a direct insult to the gods and Pele in particular.

What irony that his kinolau, changeling form, body was that of a pig! It is believed he did it out of spite and delighted in getting even with Pele for rejecting his romantic advances. Getting hanged, drawn, and quartered by the lunatic hunter was worth the risk.

But this time, the relentless pursuit by the hunter had left Kamapuaʻa feeling his age. The multiple bruises, cuts, burns, bites, and stings, though numerous, were the least of his ailments. His massive weight and poor condition agitated his liver, spleen, and kidney functions not to mention his ulcers that were acting up again and the gout in his right hoof throbbed horribly.

But the thing that irritated him the most was the boil on his rump and the poison oozing from the glanced arrow wound on his shoulder. Seeing a patch of plantain leaves, Kamapuaʻa first ate his fill of Laukahi to ease his burning ulcer in his stomach. Then he dropped on all fours and rolled over the Laukahi plant patch rubbing and mashing the Laukahi leaves with his massive back until the plantain leaves oozed forth its healing juices. With the agility and skill of a rat, Kamapuaʻa positioned his shoulder over the plant to absorb the purifying juices so that it would purge the poison from the wound.

Now if only he could get a leaf to stick to the boil on his rump, its drawing power would surely rid him of the pesky boil once and for all. But uwē, alas, it was not to be. Poetic justice was his to suffer for the boil was positioned in such a place that was truly a pain in his ʻēlemu, butt.

Laukahi: Photo taken in Pauoa Valley. This plant brings back memories of mom wilting Laukahi leaves on the stove then placing it on a boil and securing it with a bandage. The suction power of the plant draws the boil to the surface for an easy extraction.

Laukahi

TONIC
Blood purifier,
boils, stings, pus,
sterilizer, bites,
fatty liver, purifier,
cuts, absorbent,
gout, fever,
infections, blood,
shingles, wounds,
rash, ulcers, burns,
lung congestion,
weak kidney,
dehydrator,
mental illness,
poor circulation.

CONFLICT
Frustration,
seething anger.

SPIRITUAL
Ward off the
evil spirits.

It is said: The lovely Luika spent much of her day near the coral reef and shorelines playing with the tiny creatures that lived in the tide pools. But most of all, she loved to see her own reflection in the tide pool as she combed her hair. "Indeed, you are beautiful," Loli said to the startled Luika who was instantly drawn to the handsome stranger. He told her he was a Kupua, a demigod, and that their union was inevitable. "But I am promised to another," Luika protested. Loli smiled and whispered a Hūnā oli, secret entrapment spell, into her ear instantly enslaving her. "When you hear my call, you will come to me," he said and suddenly disappeared.

Luika looked about but all she saw was a lowly sea slug. Luika had trouble sleeping that night and many nights that followed. She began to waste away suffering from a loss of appetite and spending nearly all of her time at the beach well into the night.

These hō'ailona, signs, alerted her brothers who decided to follow her to see if their suspicions were right. Knowing that she was strongly drawn to the tide pools, they hid themselves near the reef prior to sunset and waited. As they suspected, Loli, a sea slug, emerged from the tide pool and transformed into a handsome young man. Minutes later, Luika appeared and helplessly fell into his arms spellbound by the changeling's chant. "Ino ho'okalakupua, wicked magic," one brother whispered angrily. "He has enchanted her. We must break the kapu, spell."

As her brothers watched, Luika was held captive till dawn and released only after the Kupua had fully pleasured himself. As the morning sun rose, the Kupua began to change back into its animal form, the most dangerous and vulnerable time for the demigod and exactly the opportunity the brothers were waiting for. As the Kupua transformed, so great was their anger that the brothers speared, sliced, diced, and shredded the sea slug into a thousand pieces. Gathering the shredded pieces, they took them home, cooked, and ate it with great relish! But uwē, alas, one shredded piece was left behind and magically regenerated itself. "Revenge is mine," the mangled Kupua angrily spewed as it crept into a tide pool and disappeared. 'Ōlelo no'eau, there is a saying, "Ho'omalu na keiki, o Hawai'i, protect the children of Hawai'i." Be vigilant as Loli still lurks about disguised in many different forms.

Loli: Photo taken at the Waikiki Aquarium. Spooky legends proved most effective in making children aware of their surroundings. "Don't trust strangers, and never go out alone," were important cultural themes.

Loli

TONIC
Sex stimulant,
infertility,
weak kidney,
bladder,
muscle, cancer,
swollen joints,
pain, tired blood,
dehydration,
fungus, sterilizer,
infection,
weak immune system.

CONFLICT
Lust, fear,
vanity, anxiety,
obsession,
low self-esteem,
perfectionist.

MOʻOLELO: LEGEND of MAʻO
Cotton, *Gossypium sandvicense*

It is said: Chief Kualiʻi was now 102 years old. The absence of desire to spread his royal seed became a family concern, for this chief was most beloved. All of his Pua Aliʻi, his royal children, were revered and prized as mates because longevity was in their bones. But uwē, alas, Kualiʻi had not produced an heir in a number of years causing great concern.

He secretly complained to his Kahuna Lāʻau lapaʻau, personal herbalist, of constant stomach cramps and leg muscle spasms that often woke him up in the middle of the night. The chief also complained about having to constantly urinate more times a day than he could count. These miserable health issues depressed the chief to the point of causing a lackluster desire to mate.

The Kahuna Lāʻau lapaʻau instructed the family to serve the chief fresh Maʻo, cotton, blossoms with each meal to remedy the situation. As expected, the healing process of consuming cotton blossoms was methodically slow and languishing. The Gods finally smiled upon the beloved aging Chief. The makahiki season of celebration had begun. Freedom, music, and games provided the right romantic atmosphere. When the wet season ended, the youngest Chieftess of the court proudly displayed her ʻŌpū, tummy, in full bloom.

This Pua Aliʻi, this royal child, was the last to be born from the loins of Chief Kualiʻi. At the age of 27, this young man knelt at his dying father's side and received the last "Hā mauli ola, breath of life," from his 175-year old father, Chief Kualiʻi.

Maʻo: Photo taken at Waikahalulu Falls Garden. This legend was created from historical information provided by Abraham Fornander concerning the health of King Kualiʻi.

Maʻo

TONIC
Sex stimulant,
stomach
cramps,
spasms,
swollen
glands,
cancer,
tumors,
swelling,
bacteria,
infection,
relaxant,
fatigue,
rejuvenator,
depression.

CONFLICT
Lust,
pride,
indolence,
helplessness,
anxiety.

MO'OLELO: LEGEND OF MAI'A
Banana, *Musa paradisaca*

It is said: It was La'i, the lusty demigod, who desired the lovely Princess Keali'iwahilani and could not resist the beauty of the mortal maiden.

Being a demigod with supernatural powers, La'i transformed himself as a bright yellow fruit, luscious, aromatic, and sweet yet firm to the touch. This was the first time the Princess had seen this edible fruit. Up until now, her diet consisted of fresh fish and sweet Poi. The fruit so fascinated Keali'iwahilani that at the end of the day, she decided not to eat the fruit but would keep it until the next morning. She placed it near her sleeping mat for safekeeping and fell asleep.

It was during that deep dark night, La'i savagely took Keali'iwahilani against her will. Her stifled cries of terror went helpless into the night. Why had the Gods abandoned her? How did she offend them? Shameful guilt and terror filled her mind and heart.

Even more offensive, nine months to the day, the distraught Princess gave birth to an E'epa, a gelatinous formed baby. This lustful act of La'i infuriated the Gods. Rather than have this abomination wander the earth as half-god half-mortal, they transformed the E'epa child into useless Limu u'a'u'a, seaweed.

From that time forward, kanaka maoli, Native Hawaiian, women were forbidden to eat the fruit and were told never to sleep with a banana near their beds.

Mai'a: Photo taken in Pauoa Valley. Ravaging a princess or a maiden in distress are common themes that inspire legends such as this one.

Mai‘a

TONIC
Asthma, thrush,
constipation, impotency,
tension, germs,
infection, virus,
poison.

CONFLICT
Anxiety,
fear,
terror,
guilt,
self-esteem,
shame,
lust,
self-pity,
helplessness.

MO'OLELO: LEGEND of MĀMAKI
Tea, *Pipturus albidus*

It is said: the Princess Ruth Ke'elikōlani was ridden with gout and arthritis caused by a cuddled lifestyle and by the ardent love of her people who constantly fed her the richest of foods in the kingdom of Hawai'i.

One day, the princess noticed that the eldest of her handmaids with the knurliest arthritic fingers went happily going about her chores pain free and with great ease. Now Princess Ruth had been suffering from an array of physical problems which included arthritis and wondered what her handmaid's health secret was. "Māmaki Tea," the matron replied.

The Princess was stunned by the answer. "Māmaki is used to make Kapa cloth and brewed as a tea during the birthing process," the Princess countered.

"'Ae, yes," the handmaid humbly replied. "But it is also good for blood pressure problems. Māmaki also strengthens the immune system and cleans the stomach, liver, colon, bladder, bowels, voids diabetes, and helps to relieve the pain of arthritis." The handmaid chattered on and on convincing the Princess of the extended healing properties of Māmaki Tea.

From that day on, Māmaki Tea became the most favorite tea to serve iced on a hot summer's day and was always on Princess Ruth's table.

Māmaki: Photo Photo taken at Ho'omaluhia Botanical Park. This legend was inspired by my cousin Lani Kiesel who went everywhere with me looking for the herbs in this book. Whenever we drove by Central Intermediate School, Lani would reminisce about her Great, Great, Great Aunty Princess Ruth Luka Keanolani Kauanahoahoa Keoelikōlani who once lived on the site.

Māmaki

TONIC
Regulates blood pressure,
removes fatty toxins from the blood,
strengthens the immune system,
stomach, liver,
colon,
bladder,
bowel problems,
weak kidneys,
stiff joints,
body fluid
stagnation.

CONFLICT
Gluttony,
envy,
pride,
indolence.

MO'OLELO: LEGEND of NAUPAKA KAHAKAI & KUAHIWI
Fan Flower, *Scaevola Sericea, & Chamissoniana*

It is said: With their visions clouded by anger and ancient family vengeance and mistrust, opposing families bitterly tore apart two young lovers entrapping them in an endless and futile family feud. Their heartening pleas that their love and joy could heal both families were scorned and belittled as immature infatuation.

The beautiful maiden Kahakai was forced to live by the sea, and Kuahiwi, her true love, was banished to the uplands above Kaimuki.

Kahakai tore a Naupaka blossom in half as a symbol of their broken hearts giving her lover one half and herself the other and vowing that the bush would only bloom half a blossom from that day forward until they were united once more. As fate would have it, the young lovers never saw each other again.

Till this day, the Naupaka Kahakai bush bares a half blossom in memory of the war-torn lovers. Yet when it is coupled with its distant Naupaka Kuahiwi, a related species of the uplands, a petal perfect flower appears. It is believed that each time these flowers are united so are the spirits of the war-torn lovers, who with gratitude, release pure love and joy upon the earth.

Naupaka Kahakai: Photo taken at Waikiki Beach. **Naupaka Kuahiwi:** Photo taken at Volcanoes National Park.

Naupaka
Kahakai

TONIC

Sore throat,
mucus,
colon infection,
lymph nodes,
nearsightedness,
farsightedness,
cross-eyed,
blurry vision,
clouded eye lens,
eye pressure,
sty,
mucous,
phlegm.

CONFLICT

Helplessness,
resentment,
anger,
frustration,
abuse,
neglect,
jealousy.

MOʻOLELO: LEGEND of NĪOI
Chile Pepper, *Capsicum Annuum*

It is said: The snow goddess Poliʻahu yearned for her lover to linger longer on his visits. But her icy body, though very beautiful, chilled him to the bone. The handsome Chief Aiwohikupua would spend a week with her, but the cold encounters forced him to return to the island of Kauaʻi to recuperate.

Fair weather permitting, sailing between islands took several weeks. Once on shore, it took Chief Aiwohikupua another week of hiking to get to the snow-capped mountains of Mauna Kea.

Upon each departure, Chief Aiwohikupua promised a quick return. But days would pass leaving the snow goddess Poliʻahu to worry. Was she not beautiful enough for him to stay with her despite the cold? Was her rival Pele, the Fire Goddess, more to his liking?

Jealousy seeped into her heart and the frustration of not knowing when he would return caused her body to grow even colder. But all her fears and worries melted away at the first sight of Aiwohikupua. As they embraced, his warm body melted the jealousy that filled the heart of the snow goddess.

This time, though it was different, Poliʻahu noticed that her lover's appearance looked vibrant and radiant and he was extra warm to the touch. She queried, "what was his secret?" The handsome chief smiled and told Poliʻahu his mother had created a protective breast and foot padding made from Kapa cloth and impregnated it with mashed Nīoi. It was the heat warming Chile Pepper poultice that kept him warm allowing him to prolong his stay with his beloved snow goddess on the snowcapped mountains of Mauna Kea.

Nīoi: Photo taken in the backyard. Legends of sibling rivalry involving Pele and her sister Poliʻahu the Snow Queen continues to evolve.

Nīoi

TONIC
Circulation,
sex stimulant,
heart stimulant,
frostbite,
artery blockages,
high blood pressure,
bleeding,
blood thinner,
stroke,
stomach issues,
gas,
congestion,
appetite,
sweating,
ulcers,
poor circulation.

CONFLICT
Anger,
worry,
frustration,
jealousy.

MO'OLELO: LEGEND of NIU
Coconut, Tree of Life, *Cocos nicifera*

It is said: The tree of life, the coconut, will feed, clothe, and watch over you. Kū, Kāne, Lono, and Kanaloa gave the coconut three eyes which are represented by three indentations on the hard, inner nut enveloped by a fibrous husk.

Each of the eyes has a specific function: one looks to the left, one looks to the right, and the third one looks down to make sure there is no one below when it decides to fall to the ground.

Falling coconuts are often heard but never felt. When a coconut, on a rare and freak occasion, falls on someone's head, islanders nod affirming that the Gods are teaching that person a lesson of Ha'aha'a, humbleness, because that person is too Pa'akiki, hard headed and stubborn.

Polynesians believe the coconut tree is a spiritual manifestation of the four major demigods Kū, Kāne, Lono and Kanaloa. Eating the fruit not only nourishes but spiritually unites the humanity with God.

The coconut tree is treasured as the "Tree of Life" throughout Polynesia. The four demigods unified in its creation to provide Kanaka Maoli, the people of Hawai'i, with a plant that would provide their every need; food, medicine, clothing, housing, bedding, flooring, canoe sails, boats, bindings, rope, utensils, cups, and more.

In the past, a coconut tree was planted at the time of birth to ensure a child would be provided for life. This tradition was mandated by the Gods throughout Polynesia and respectfully adhered to. But uwē, alas, not anymore. Sadly, another tradition disregarded and presently slipping away. The four layers of the Coconut symbolizes the manifested form of the four Demigods: Kāne, Kū, Lono and Kanaloa. Kāne is recognized as the outer husk of the whole nut itself; Kū is represented by the inner hard shell; Lono is the white meat of the coconut; and Kanaloa, the giver of life and death, is signified by the purified coconut water.

As a note of historical interest, this pure life-giving water was used by the military in World War II as a substitute for plasma.

Niu: Photo taken in Pauoa Valley. Another urban legend that continues to stand the test of time.

Niu

TONIC
Plasma, cold sores,
parasite, flu, cancer,
sterilizer, germs,
ulcers, fatigue,
eyes-ears-throat-nose
issues,
virus, skin blemishes,
infections,
ringworms, pimples,
fungus, obesity, liver,
stroke, aging,
brittle bones,
wrinkles, gout,
enlarged veins, rash,
dandruff, bladder, memory, allergy.

CONFLICT
Anger, frustration, pride, foolishness,
stubbornness,
self-pity.

SPIRITUAL USE
Symbolic unified image of the four
demigods
Kū, Kāne, Lono, Kanaloa.

MO'OLELO: LEGEND of NONI NĀMAKA O HINA
Noni Apple, Eyes of Hina, *Moronda Citrifolia*

It is said: Hina, on hearing the tragic news that her son Māui was in mortal danger, shifted into one of her kinolau, changeling body forms, as a buoyant Noni, sour apple, with many eyes. This shape enabled her to float on the ocean throughout the Pacific Islands in search of her beloved son. As she traveled, she left Noni apple seeds that magically sprouted on each isle she visited saving Hina from the error of searching that island twice.

As fate would have it, one day a village boy from a remote island went canoe fishing. He had never seen a Noni apple before and pulled it out of the water into his canoe. Much to his surprise, the fruit changed into the goddess Hina. The goddess asked the boy if he had seen her son Māui the great warrior. "'Ae, yes," the boy exclaimed, telling Hina of the great battle that took place and how a giant octopus sucked the lifegiving breath out of her son or so it seemed. "Show me where he is," Hina pleaded, "There is little time left to call his spirit back," she said.

Upon finding her son, Hina transformed herself back into a Noni fruit and instantly rooted herself in the soil next to her son. A huge tree with wide, glossy leaves bloomed. The tree set free its wide, glossy green leaves that gently floated down and covered her son's comatose body. The warmth of his mother's mystical force and pure love saturated the Noni leaves. Hina then mingled it with a restoration prayer to bring Maui back to life.

To nourish his weakened body, Hina mashed the Noni fruit and fed it to her son. It hydrated his body, moisturizing and nourishing every blood vessel, tendon, sinew, muscle, bone and strengthened his immune system increasing his life force. The Noni fruit healed his battle wounds, cuts, and sores. It also purged the pesky parasites that plagued his weak stomach. This amazing fruit went on to clear his urinary tract and normalized his vacillating blood pressure. Once he was restored to perfect health, Hina and Māui left the island but not before giving the boy that helped her a Noni apple to plant and the knowledge on how to medicinally use it. Undoubtedly, a gift of gratitude from Hina to all humanity. Till this day, the many eyes of Hina are notably visible on the Noni Apple. Its healing properties ever ready to heal and save a life.

Noni Nāmaka o Hina: Photo taken in Manoa Valley. Uncle Willie tried to get mom to coax me into drinking the stuff for my asthma.

Noni
Nāmaka o Hina

TONIC

Asthma,
tuberculosis,
diabetes, malaria,
hair loss,
high or low blood pressure,
depression,
cancer,
addictions,
flu, cuts, ulcers, arthritis, sores,
weak immune system,
infections, burns,
sluggish bowels,
infertility,
parasites,
internal balance,
adapt, align.

CONFLICT

Repression,
anger, fear,
envy,
danger,
indecisive.

MOʻOLELO: LEGEND of ʻOHE
Bamboo, *Schizostachyum glaucifolium*

It is said: Mele came often to the ʻOhe, bamboo, grove to relieve her asthmatic condition and to strengthen her weak lungs by chanting.

The ʻOhe, bamboo, grove provided the most intensified quantity of oxygen of all the plants in Hawaiʻi. The sound of the four winds singing through the branches and leaves instantly relieved stress and restored calmness which also presented the perfect setting to Noho pū, meditate and contemplate.

Here, Kanaka Maoli, the natives of Hawaiʻi, came to release their anxieties allowing their worries to drift and float ever upwards nestling on the top of the rustling leaves high above the canopy. It was believed that when spring came the four winds would combine swirling all the leaves of the entire ʻOhe grove causing them to fall in unison. As it did, Au Makua Mauloa, the Eternal Parent, in a spiritual cleansing act, would gather all the Ino and Pilikia, evil and troubles, of the entire area in one swoop releasing the leaves of their burden sending the spent leaves to the forest floor to regenerate the bamboo grove once more.

One day, the winds gently blew through the bamboo grove and Mele thought she heard Akau, the North wind, whisper to her, "Hūūūūūūūū," and so she answered, "I am Mele." "Eeeeeeee," Komohana, the West wind, happily sighed.

Mele continued, "I am here to learn all there is to know." "Uuuuuuuu," Kona Hema the South wind blew. "How can I acquire Hoʻomālamalama, enlightenment?" Mele humbly asked. "Hāāāāāāāā, breathe," Hikina the East wind softly replied. "Noho pū, meditate, and enlightenment will be yours."

Here is where the Gods spoke to humanity, and humanity in return honored their presence with music and song fashioning wind instruments out of bamboo: the ʻOhe hano, nose flute, the Kāʻekeʻeke, bamboo pipes, and the Pūʻili, split bamboo implement. These instruments are evidence of the once common practice of seeking Hoʻomālamalama, enlightenment, in the peaceful bamboo groves of Hawaiʻi.

ʻOhe: Photo taken at Kaniakapūpū bamboo forest near King Kalakaua hunting lodge.

'Ohe

TONIC
Kidney,
urinary infections,
bleeding,
phlegm, asthma,
cloudy and dry eye conditions,
congested stomach and
bowels,
fatty liver and blood vessels,
cancer, weight loss,
virus, digestion,
clogged artery.

CONFLICT
Anxiety,
abandonment,
confused,
baffled,
perplexed.

SPIRITUAL USE
Trap evil spirits,
induce euphoria using bamboo
flute and other bamboo instruments.

It is said: ʻŌhiʻa, a handsome young warrior of Puna, spurned the affections of the Fire Goddess Pele. It was rumored the Fire Goddess, in a fit of rage, turned ʻŌhiʻa into a fruit tree and hid him in the Puna rainforest where she held him against his will. As he stood helpless, Pele would caress the fruit tree that held ʻŌhiʻa captive licking it with lustful tongues of fire and drinking the succulent juice the fruit bared.

The heat parched his skin drying him to the core, and her lustful appetite drained and weakened his life force. How he longed to see his beloved maiden Lehua once more. Her voice was all that kept him alive. He had heard her calls as she wandered through the forest in search of him. "If only she would come this way," ʻŌhiʻa wishfully thought.

While thoughts of being found filled ʻŌhiʻa with hope, helpless thoughts filled the mind of Lehua. What chance could a lowly maiden have against the Fire Goddess Pele. Yet filled with fear, Lehua somehow found the courage to wander deeper and deeper into the Puna rainforest in search of ʻŌhiʻa. Hunger and exhaustion persuaded Lehua to rest under a magnificent tree laden with fruit. She reached up, picked a fruit, and ate it. The subtle scent of the fruit reminded her of ʻŌhiʻa. It was then she realized she had found her true love, but her joy quickly turned into fear as Pele suddenly appeared.

Lehua begged the Fire Goddess Pele to release him and change ʻŌhiʻa back into a man again pointing out that he was just a mere mortal unbefitting of a goddess. Out of spite Pele refused. "He is mine," she said, "you shall never see him again!" Pele maliciously laughed and disappeared. The thought of never seeing ʻŌhiʻa again fatally crushed Lehua. Clinging to the fruit tree, she died of a broken heart.

As fate would have it, the plea of the poor maiden caught the ear and touched the heart of her personal Awaikū, guardian. Knowing the spell casted by the Fire Goddess Pele could not be reversed, her Awaikū changed the maiden's spirit into a clinging flower that would appear on the tree trunk once a year allowing the lovers to perpetually embrace in spite of the Fire Goddess Pele. Unquestionably, the fruit and flowers of the ʻŌhiʻaʻai tree is the glorious personification of love in bloom.

ʻŌhiʻaʻai: Photo taken off of the Pali Road and Booth Road. Much of Hawaiian folklore is steeped in magic such as the case and legend of ʻŌhiʻaʻai, mountain apple tree and its blossom.

'Ōhiʻaʻai

TONIC
Afterbirth tonic,
lubricant,
moisturizer,
fertility problems,
internal congestion,
impotency,
tuberculosis,
bronchitis,
dry-mouth,
dehydration,
congestion,
problems.

CONFLICT
Helplessness,
repressed anger,
envy,
lust,
sorrow,
pride.

MO'OLELO: LEGEND of 'ŌLENA
Ginger, Turmeric, *Curcuma domestica*

It is said: From the grave, Peleuli yearned for her great, great, great, granddaughter Lauoho o Pele and beaconed her from beyond the veil. The child drifted in a twilight state lingering dangerously between life and death; her spirit teetering like a balloon on a string high above her body causing her blood to nearly boil on numerous occasions baffling the medical doctors. It would be only a matter of time before the Aka cord, soul linkage, would be severed and the child's soul would be released into the keeping of her dearly departed great, great, great, Queen grandmother. But there were greater forces of love on Earth that battled for the child's spirit.

First and foremost, to save the child the Queen's name had to be 'Oki, severed, to completely disconnect the child from Queen Peleuli. Removing the given Hawaiian name that spiritually attached her to the departed Queen was crucial, an exceedingly difficult and dangerous task. This act was crucial for it was the only way the drifting spirit could be called back into the child's body and stabilized permanently. The following sacred prayer to call back a drifting spirit was graciously given for publication by Aunty Momi Ruane for the sake of prosperity and in memory of Tutu Kamanu.

"E ke akua, 'i nana kalani ame ka honua ame na pauloa. 'Olu 'olu oe, e ho'i ho'i mai ka 'uhane o Lauoho o Pele. E ho'opa'a hoa pili iho me kona kino. A'ole ae i kona 'uhane e awana. Mana, i puka hale, o ka ili honua nei. "God, who created the heavens and the earth and all living things, please bring back the spirit of Lauoho o Pele and put it back in the body and don't let it wander from here."

Such a prayer was continuously repeated as the child was sprinkled with a spring of 'Ōlena leaf dipped in a glass of Wai ho'āno, holy water, Pa'akai, sea salt, and a piece of 'Ōlena, ginger root. The child was then encouraged to sip the salt water and to chew a piece of 'Ōlena root from the bottom of the glass. The act of chewing the 'Ōlena root spiritually anchored the soul back into its natural position tucked under the Houpo, solar plexus. The proper offerings and apologies were made along with a stern warning; the life of the child was not to be taken under any circumstances, namesake or not. Life was to be lived to the fullest to increase the knowledge of the soul and not to be interfered with until it had its fill and its last breath given according to the agreement between that soul and Au Makua Mauloa, the Eternal Parent. What happened to the child? She lived to be 79 years old giving up her mauli hā, soul's departing breath, in the presence of her sons and daughter, the author of this book.

'Ōlena: Photo taken at Hawai'i Tropical Botanical Garden. 'Ōlena requires rainforest conditions which makes it difficult to find. Tutu Kamanu and Aunty Momi Ruane were great herbalist and spiritual healers, each in her own right. Both used this herb accordingly.

ʻŌlena

TONIC
Cancer, tumor,
fatty liver,
congestion,
poor appetite,
circulation,
tired blood,
constipation,
parasites,
indigestion,
nausea,
breathless,
strokes,
heart ailments.

CONFLICT
Stagnation,
anger, envy,
pride, lust.

SPIRITUAL USE
Spiritual
purification,
grounding.

MO'OLELO: LEGEND of PA'AKAI
Sea Salt, *Sodium chloride*

It is said: Hōkūlaʻa ʻehu hated to tend the family salt beds at Hānāpepe. "Why me, Tūtū, Grandma?" Hōkūlaʻa ʻehu complained. "Our family has been honored as one of the forty-seven to mālama, to care, these sacred sea salt beds, that's why," Tūtū replied.

"Why is this place sacred? It looks like dirty salt to me." "'Ae, yes, that is why it is so sacred," Tūtū continued. "Do you know your name tells the story of our existence?" Tūtū said as she carefully raked the crystallized salt. "Come Hōkūlaʻa ʻehu, look," she said and carefully picked up a crystallized piece of salt that looked like the backbone of a prehistoric animal.

"Nānā i ke kumu, look to the source," she said. "You see this? All the stars in the sky are made of salt crystals." Then Tūtū picked up some red dirt that formed the banks of the salt beds and fondled it with her fingers. "This is the other half of the story. Mix them together and you get Nui manu, humanity. You and me and all humanity are created from the dust of the stars and the dirt of this land."

"Not!" Hōkūlaʻa ʻehu expressed half believing Tūtū. "'Ae, yes, our body is made up of the dust and salt from the heavens and the dirt of the earth. We must eat sea salt to sustain life," she continued. "Our 'Ohana, family, was blessed with the honor of sustaining the lives of our people. Without salt, we could not dry and preserve our food for the lean times. Without salt, we could not clean out our 'Ōpū, stomach. Our keiki, children, could suffer deformities. Without salt, our teeth would fall out and we would age before our time. Without salt, we could not be spiritually cleansed and bless our homes and ourselves."

"Nough Tūtū, I get the pitcha," the boy said nodding his head exhibiting enlightened wisdom. "Give me the rake." That day, Hōkūlaʻa ʻehu grew into his name: ***Sacred Reddish Brown Stardust.***

Pa'akai: Photo taken when visiting the Mana Salt Ponds on Kaua'i. Legend inspired by Au Makua mauloa.

Pa'akai

TONIC
Preservative,
purgative,
clears nose and throat congestion,
helps to prevent deformities and
tooth decay,
premature aging,
skin disorders,
allergies,
regulate hydration.

CONFLICT
Anger,
Indolence.

SPIRITUAL USE
Spiritual cleansing
and protection.

MOʻOLELO: LEGEND of PEPEIAO
Tree Ears, Wood Fungus, *Polypore*

It is said: Kumu hula, Pepe had wandered into the forest and laid himself against an old decaying tree trunk. He knew his time had come and wanted to spend his Mauli hā ola, last breath, chanting to his beloved goddess Laka. Wheezing and panting, he began to Oli his chant of praise and uwē, alas, the goddess herself appeared. "Oh, if only I was younger my song to you would be so much more the pure," the old man wheezed. With the wave of her hand, the goddess Laka sprinkled what looked like sand over the trunk of the tree he was leaning on. As he watched, each granule blossomed into what he thought looked like ears.

"Take and eat," the goddess encouraged. It was bitter and hard to chew but the old Kumu humbly did as he was told and uwē, alas, he felt the mana, energy, from the plant surge into his body invigorating him. The flood of mana warmed his weary bones and energized the blood in his veins. He could actually feel the tight pain squeezing his heart subside, and the arthritis in his knees and hands that had ended his days as a kumu hula, dance instructor, temporarily disappeared.

Kumu Pepe felt like a young man again. Getting up on his feet and with deep bended knees, he began his ʻAi haʻa, with great verbose, chanting his special oli of love, gratitude, and adoration for his aumakua Laka, the goddess of the forest. At the end, the exhausted Pepei leaned against the old tree and released his last breath. As he did, the goddess Laka snatched his departing spirit and infused it with the strange ear-like plant.

"You have soothed and warmed the chambers of my heart," she said. And then mandated, "From this day forward, these shall be called Pepeiao in memory of the one that loved me so. These, too, shall honor all kumu hula for it is they that keep me alive. In the presence of these ears I hear all who come to the forest."

Till this day when Pepeiao ears are seen in the forest, Laka, Pepe, and all kumu hula are called into remembrance and respectfully honored.

Pepeiao: Photo taken in Nuʻuanu Valley. In memory of my favorite Kumu Hula Ellsworth Noa, Kumu Hula Kuʻulei Punua, and Kumu Hula Maiʻki Aiu Lake. Each inspired and trained this Pākiki (stubborn) kid to hula.

Pepeiao

TONIC
Fights cancer,
virus, tumor,
bacteria,
tinnitus,
purgative,
inflammation,
arthritis,
liver cleanse,
diabetes,
tired blood,
immune system,
congestion.

CONFLICT
Envy, pride,
anger, greed.

SPIRITUAL USE
Spiritual unity, body, mind, and soul
coherence, hallucinogenic..

MOʻOLELO: LEGEND of PLUMERIA
Frangipani, *Plumeria ruba*

It is said: Kana, a young man, suffered from a constant occurrence of sty in his right eye. No matter what medication or how many times he had the sty lanced and drained, it always came back. Finally, Tūtū took Kana to go see Aunty Kina for she would know what to do. Everyone enjoyed visiting Aunty Kina. The scent of flowers wafting throughout her home was a pleasant experience enjoyed by all. Well, almost all. The scent of flowers immediately repulsed Kana who, for quite a while, could not wear a scented flower lei, garland. This major objection to flowers alerted Aunty Kina to his mysterious condition. Using her gift of ʻIke pāpālua, second sight, she could see that an ʻUhane makā ʻeo, "angry eye," was sitting on his shoulder watching her through the young man's right eye holding its nose repulsed by the smell of the flowers in her home.

Aunty Kina told the young man to wait, and she went into her garden. She eventually returned with four Plumeria leaves and a beautiful Lei. She instructed Kana to look directly into her eyes, and as he did, she tore up the first leaf in the front of him and loudly commanded the angry spirit in his eye to leave. "You know how sore this ʻae lāʻau, sap, going be?" she said menacingly ripping the second and third leaves. Both leaves began dripping white gooey sap. "If you don't leave," she threatened again, "I going poke your eye with this!" she said shaking the fourth leaf at the sty hitting Kana on the right shoulder with the leaf to make good, her threat.

Kana flinched from the action of being symbolically whipped on the shoulder, and as he jerked, Aunty commanded the ʻUhane makā ʻeo to "hele wale aku lā, go into the light, and ʻAʻole mai, never come back." She then graced Kana with a flower lei and gave him instructions on how to cook and eat the flowers. "Plumeria!" Kana protested, "That's graveyard flower!" Kana voiced with incredulous surprise, "you sure can eat this?" "ʻAe," Aunty replied, "make ʻono pūpū, delicious appetizers."

Aunty went on to say that Plumeria protects and wards off pesky spirits that cling and feed off of angry energy that oozes from the eye. She also gave him ash powder made from the sap of the Plumeria blossom to put on his swollen eyelid. "You put a little on the lump every day till it melts away!" she firmly instructed. "So, no looking at other people with Makā ʻeo, angry eyes, or the sty going come back!" aunty sternly warned. Pointing to the sty on his eyelid, Aunty continued, "No more jealousy, no more envy, and no more resentment. These ugly thoughts weaken the body letting ʻUhane makā ʻeo take up residence in your eye." The last thing Kana remembered and will never forget is Aunty Kina calling after him as he left her house, "No more stink eye!"

Plumeria: Photo taken at Waialua Plantation. Legend inspired by the beauty and aroma of this plant

Plumeria

TONIC
Aromatherapy,
fever,
diarrhea,
virus,
sty,
detoxification,
lung and nose
congestion,
warts, sores, bumps,
food delicacy.

CONFLICT
Envy,
jealousy,
anger, greed,
resentment.

SPIRITUAL USE
Spiritual protection,
dislodging uninvited spirits.

MOʻOLELO: LEGEND OF POHĀ
Gooseberry, Musk Tomato, Chinese Lantern, *Physalis peru viana*

It is said: Kaohu was worried as he hurried along the old King's Highway in Puna. "Not so fast Iʻaokepa," Kaohu complained. "The Night Marchers walk this Ala nui, roadway, on the Night of Kāne, bro, and that's tonight!" Iʻaokepa scoffed, "That old story, nobody believes that anymore." Suddenly, up ahead on the trail, a band of warriors walking four abreast and several inches off the ground came towards them bearing torches and chanting a spine chilling oli, chant. "It's them," Kaohu gasped. "Quick, strip your clothes off and lay down face up like a dead man," Kaohu whispered. "Whatever you do, don't move or open your eyes." Iʻaokepa needn't be told twice for he too had heard of the Night Marchers and what must be done to survive an encounter with them.

Both men could feel the icy cold breath of the marchers passing right over them. Iʻaokepa warily turned his head to one side trying hard to resist the urge to peek. But he couldn't help himself and slowly opened one eye. He was surprised to see a reflection of himself in a Pohā berry dangling from a bush in the moonlight. Other berries came into view, each one looking like a little lantern mystically reflecting its surroundings.

Suddenly a ghostly image appeared staring into the berry right at him! "AAAAAAAAAAAAAAAAAH!!!" both Iʻaokepa and the ghost screamed in surprise; the ghost for seeing itself for the first time causing it to vanish and Iʻaokepa for seeing the Night Marcher up close and personal.

Everything that followed after that was a blur. Iʻaokepa could only remember running for his life, naked in the moonlight, with Kaohu hot on his heels. Ghostly voices were yelling in the background, "Kuʻi, Kuʻi, Strike, Strike!" then another voice that sounded like the dearly departed grandfather of Kaohu yelling back, "'Aʻole, no, mine, mine!"

This was the ghastly story the two cousins were relating in full detail to the spellbound family members gathered around the pakaukau, table. Just then, Tūtū, Grandma, put a huge bowl of Pohā berries on the table. Kaohu jumped to his feet. "Pohā, Pohā, this is what saved our lives!" he gasped. "'Aʻole, no," Tūtū said. "It was your dearly departed grandfather." Tūtū continued, "Pohā is good medicine though good for thinning the blood, asthma attacks, headaches, infections, but best of all," Tūtū smiled, "Meaʻai, dessert!" "'Ai, 'ai, eat, eat," Tutu smiled.

Pohā: Photo taken at Hawaiʻi Volcanoes National Park. Urban legends of "night marchers" continue to flourish with countless encounters.

Pohā

TONIC
Blood thinner,
virus, fever,
toxins, mucus,
chills, fatigue,
night sweats,
bone and joint pain,
headache, stress,
gonorrhea, asthma,
infection,
purgative, weakness,
easy bruising or bleeding,
appetite or
weight loss,
cramps,
swelling, pain,
diabetes.

CONFLICT
Anger, gluttony,
lust, fear,
helplessness

MO'OLELO: LEGEND of PŌPOLO
Black Nightshade, *Solanum americanum*

It is said: Lono, a much beloved chief of Ka'u on the island of Hawai'i, severely injured his foot with his O'opahu, digging stick. The wound instantly filled with mud from the Kalo, taro, patch that he was standing in. Though his subjects tried their best to clean the wound, they could not prevent the gangrenous infection that drained his life force and threatened the survival of their beloved chief. Lono was angry and frustrated for being so careless and resigned himself to his fate.

As the Gods would have it, Kamakanui'ahailono, the first Kahuna Lā'au lapa'au, herbalist, to ever walk the land of Hawai'i, had come in pursuit of malicious spreading disease carriers from a distant land. Kamakanui'ahailono had hopes of overtaking and subduing them from further spreading illness throughout the islands.

The reputation of Kahuna Kamakanui'ahailono preceded him. His services were immediately implored by the faithful servants of Lono to heal their beloved chief. Kamakanui'ahailono agreed and made a poultice consisting of sea salt and crushed Pōpolo berries and covered the wound. In time, the wound healed, and the infection disappeared.

This miraculous event changed Chief Lonopuha forever. He became an ardent student of Kamakanui'ahailono giving up his chiefly duties to become Lonopuha, the first student to learn the magic of Lā'au lapa'au. Lonopuha recognized the value of healing with herbs and pursued its usage for the sake of his people under the watchful eyes of Kahuna Kamakanui'ahailono.

As for the Pōpolo berry, its status was promptly elevated. Once a lowly weed, the Pōpolo berry became the first treasured healing herb of Hawai'i.

Pōpolo: Photo taken at Makapu'u Point. Historical Legend Chief Lono was the first Kanaka maoli Kahuna La'au lapa'au.

Pōpolo

TONIC
Chest and lung infections,
weak immune system,
iron-poor blood,
boils,
cuts, sores, wounds,
cancer.

CONFLICT
Pride,
impatience,
anger,
anxiety,
ego,
intense vanity.

MO'OLELO: LEGEND of PUAKALA
Prickly Beach Poppy: *Argemone glauca*

It is said: The child of Puakala, a lowly handmaiden of the King, had accidentally crawled into the shadow of the Chief Wohi aka'ali'i. This act was considered an attack upon the King for no one was allowed to walk on the shadow of the King. The penalty for such a grievous act was immediate death.

Grabbing her child and shielding it under her, Puakala prostrated herself before the King and begged to spare the life of her child. "A sacred law has been broken," the attending Kahuna nui, High Priest, coldly announced. "The penalty must be paid," the Kahuna demanded. Puakala spoke quickly bargaining for her child's life. "I have the knowledge that can stop the toothache of the great, wise, and benevolent all forgiving King. Take my life instead," she begged. "A kapu has been broken the child must die," the Kahuna sternly insisted.

"Wait," the Chief commanded and reached for the child sitting the little keiki on his lap declaring, "blood of my blood, bone of my bone," immediately making the child his own. "Now go girl and get the Lā'au," the king ordered. Puakala gladly did so and came back with a thick pasty sap from a prickly poppy plant and molded it into a tiny poultice. She humbly offered it to the King suggesting that it be gently mashed into the cavity. The effects were immediate. It numbed the jaw and relieved the pain much to the great relief of the King.

"And what of the kapu," the Kahuna declared. "A life must be taken for this offense; it is divine law. No one can walk on the shadow of the King and live." Saddened by the truth, the Chief reluctantly ordered the death of Puakala in place of her child. She gladly blessed the King for sparing her child's life and allowing her to die instead. As the Lā'au Palau, war club, was raised over her head, she blessed and sang praises to the King. "Not in many a year have I seen a more faithful servant," the King lamented. "From this day forward, this flower is kapu, reserved, to be used only by royalty." In honor of the handmaiden, the saddened King named the poppy plant Puakala, the flower that forgives.

Puakala: Photo taken at Waikahalulu Falls herb garden. Rigid Royal traditions and customs inspired this legend.

Puakala

TONIC
Relaxant,
headache,
tension,
toothache,
stuffy nose,
ulcers,
physical and/or mental stress,
pain.

CONFLICT
Fearful,
uneasy,
helpless,
anxiety,
vulnerable,
defenseless,
powerless,
victimized,
apprehension.

MOʻOLELO: LEGEND of TĪ, KĪ, LĀʻĪ
Tī Leaf, Good Luck Plant, *Cordyline terminalis*

It is said: The problems that occur when trying to take raw pork over the Nuʻuanu Pali are linked to the turbulent relationship between Pele the Fire Goddess and Kamapuaʻa, the Hog demigod. Kamapuaʻa's heavy wheezing, snorting, and grunting so irritated Pele that she could barely stand the sight of him. But it was altogether different when he slipped into his handsome Kinolau, changeling form, as a sweet fragment entwining fern. In this form, he was simply irresistible to all women including Pele the Fire Goddess. Kamapuaʻa was Kolohe, very naughty. His womanizing infuriated the Fire Goddess causing her blood to boil giving Pele a bone splitting headache and a fiery scorching fever.

In a jealous rage, Pele would send hot fingers of lava over the Pali ridge into the Hog demigods' domain causing major damage to the windward side of the island. In retaliation, Kamapuaʻa would sneak over the Pali at night and dig up and devour her favorite sweet potato patches. The two were forever quarreling. Thankfully, Lono the God of Peace and Spiritual Protection was summoned to mediate for the two hot-tempered lovers. A strict Kapu, restraint, was set in place. Kamapuaʻa agreed to remain on the windward side of the Pali and Pele on the leeward side. Should this Kapu be broken, a severe reprimand would be levied by the Gods.

This is an open warning to all; never sneak raw pork over the Nuʻuanu Pali or you will risk the wrath of the Fire Goddess Pele. It is said, Pele has commanded a legion of ravaging spirits to devour any hint or form of the Hog demigod Kamapuaʻa including raw bacon.

According to a 1986 Honolulu newspaper article, had it not been for a Tī Leaf plant a soldier from Hickam Air Force Base, out to test the myth, would have fallen to his death. He was found dangling over the Pali cliff clinging to a skinny Tī Leaf plant, the Kinolau, changeling form, of Lono the God of Peace and Spiritual Protection. It took a helicopter from the Honolulu Fire Department to safely pluck the lucky soldier off the cliff.

WARNING: Never take raw pork over the Nuʻuanu Pali, but if you must, be sure to wrap it in a Lāʻī leaf bundle. Perhaps the ravaging spirits that guard the Pali Highway will think it's a gift for the Fire Goddess Pele.

Tī, Kī, Lāʻī: Photo taken in Pauoa Valley. Urban legends Pele, Kamapuaʻa, and the Pali abound. Here is another one.

Tī, Kī, Lāʻī Leaf

TONIC
Asthma, nose-bleed,
growths, fever,
headache, swelling,
fungus, asthma, virus,
coolant,
hemorrhoids,
bloody urine,
swollen gums,
sprains, toxins,
food preservative,
sterilizer,
tenderizer,
bandage, footwear,
clothing, raincoat.

CONFLICT
Anger, lust,
gluttony, indolence,
pride, envy.

SPIRITUAL USE
Spiritual protection,
spiritual blessings,
ward off evil spirits.

MO'OLELO: LEGEND of 'UALA
Sweet Potato, *Ipomoea batatas*

It is said: In order to protect her babies from Pueo, the owl, 'Iole, the rat, cleverly disguised them as 'Uala, sweet potato, vines. She would burrow holes in the potato patch and place each keiki, baby, in a hole upside down with their tails sticking out camouflaging them as 'Uala vines. 'Iole cautioned each one to be quiet and to be as still as possible until she returned from her hunt.

A flower carefully marked the spot where each of her keiki was hidden. Upon her return, 'Iole would pull her keiki out by their little tails and feed them. 'Iole constantly warned her babies not to leave the safety of the 'Uala patch and most importantly to be aware of Pueo and his deadly claws.

One day when 'Iole was away, her naughty keiki, now almost full grown, indulged in a risky game with Pueo. The little rats decided to play a nasty trick on the nearly blind, old owl. They disguised a sweet potato to look like a mouse. They chewed a hole in the back end of the potato and stuck a striped potato vine in it to make it look like a rat's rump and tail. Then they wiggled the vine until it caught Pueo, the owl's, attention.

Not realizing what it really was and thinking it was a juicy little mouse, Pueo swooped down greedily clutching and then gulping down the chunk of sweet potato. Uwē, Uwē, alas, the poor old owl retched and retched and finally vomited the chunk of 'Uala from its system leaving the owl with a terrible tummy ache and a bruised ego.

While sweet potato is a wonderful diet that strengthened little babies, it was extremely dangerous for Pueo, the owl. What is good for one animal can be deadly to another. It is no wonder why to this day, that the owl and rat remain mortal enemies.

'Uala: Photo taken in Pauoa Valley. Legend inspired by watching a Pueo, an owl, hovering above a sweet potato patch.

'Uala

TONIC
Asthma,
sleeplessness,
laxative, purgative,
sore throat,
bait,
female hormonal problems,
frailty,
strengthens elderly, vomiting.

CONFLICT
Uncertainty,
frightful,
foreboding,
menacing,
nervous, fear.

MOʻOLELO: LEGEND of ʻUHALOA, HIʻALOA
Marshmallow, *Waltheria Americana*

It is said: The night raiding cannibal warriors of Kealiʻi ai kanaka often terrorized the villagers of Waianae. These were not kanaka maoli, native Hawaiians, but people from a foreign land that made the Waianae mountain range their home.

On one such occasion, a young girl named Mala heard someone whistling outside the house and as was the custom invited the stranger to come in and eat. She was shocked by the dark shadow of a man that appeared in her doorway. Poor Mala was overpowered by the dark stranger. Her screams of horror went unanswered in the night. The dark man disappeared as quickly as he came leaving a throbbing heartbeat in her belly. Her suspicion was confirmed by Kahuna pule ike pāpālua, a praying psychic priest. Growing within her belly was a man-eating child that even now was gnawing at her Naʻau, intestines, causing her tremendous pain.

"This keiki must be removed or you will die. It cannot be allowed to walk the Earth," the Kahuna pule warned. "This baby's hunger can only be quenched by the eating of human flesh," the Kahuna said. Mala protested, "But it is the fruit of my womb." "It will be a thorn to the people in the village. You must abort the child," the Kahuna commanded. Frightened, Mala agreed and was instructed to gather several ʻUhaloa plants consisting of roots, leaves, and stalk. She was then instructed to take it to the Kahuna Lāʻau lapaʻau, herbalist, who prepared the concoction which she immediately consumed expecting to abort the child. But Uwē, alas, the Laʻau proved useless against the darkness growing within her ʻŌpū, belly. For the attempt, the child inflicted Mala with severe abdominal pains.

As the days passed, Mala was ravaged by high fevers that weakened her all the more. The rapid growth of the child drained the energy from her bones leaving her riddled with arthritis. Once a lovely woman, Mala was now gaunt and aged far beyond her years. A build-up of phlegm in her lungs caused her to suffer dreaded asthma attacks. While the ʻUhaloa helped with these debilitating secondary ailments and in keeping Mala alive, the child to everyone's amazement continued to grow despite the continual use of the highly poisonous ʻUhaloa concoction. It even increased in size reaching full maturity within 28 days. As dreaded, Mala died from childbirth ravaged from the inside out. As for the child, it was stolen away by sympathetic cannibal forces. It is rumored that the father was none other than Kealiʻi ai kanaka, the man-eating cannibal king of Waianae.

ʻUhaloa: Photo taken at Waimea Botanical Gardens. Urban Legend of Kealiʻi ai Kanaka "man-eater" still generates a spine-tingling story .

'Uhaloa Hi'aloa

TONIC
Abortion,
fatigue,
cold sore,
throat, cough,
loose bowels,
arthritis,
asthma, phlegm,
mucous, cramps,
headache,
infection,
pain, constipation.

CONFLICT
Fear,
anger,
anxiety,
helplessness,
depressed,
lonely,
abandonment,
vulnerable.

MOʻOLELO: LEGEND of ʻULU
Breadfruit, Tree of Plenty, *Artocarpus incisa*

It is said: The demigod Kū, disguised as a mortal, married the beautiful innocent maiden Mālamaʻuluʻokalani. Nine months later, Mālama gave birth to a beautiful baby boy they named ʻUlu. The child was quite sickly, weak, and suffered many physical ailments. Mālama was unaware of the fact that her baby's blood was too rich being born of a demigod and a mortal mother. She was resigned to worry constantly because ʻUlu was physically a very delicate child.

This union was an abomination to the Gods who set forth a famine that laid bare the land and polluted the sea. The famine reached epic proportions affecting all of Hawaiʻi including Mālama and her son ʻUlu who fell gravely ill from the lack of food.

Under the dire circumstances, Kū was forced to reveal himself to his wife and told her that in order to save her, their son, and the rest of the village, he would have to enter the realm of the underworld to stop the famine.

This meant that he could never return. Kū, in parting, instructed Mālamaʻuluʻokalani to mark the spot where he entered the earth and watch for a tree baring fruit of plenty. She watched with great sorrow and amazement as Kū dove headfirst into the ground and disappeared.

As Mālamaʻuluʻokalani wept bitterly, her tears fell upon the exact spot where Kū had entered the earth and instantly a tree sprouted baring an abundance of fruit just as Kū had promised. As she tenderly picked the first fruit from the tree, she heard her beloved Kū sigh a loving goodbye, "ʻUlu."

ʻUlu: Photo taken in Pauoa Valley. Legend inspired by Mary Kawena Pukui and Laura S.C. Green.

'Ulu

TONIC
Skin ailments,
fungus,
broken bones,
pinched nerves,
sciatica, sprains,
thrush,
stomach cramps,
infections,
loose bowels,
purifier,
ear infection,
purgative.

CONFLICT
Guilt,
unresolved issues,
envy,
anxiety,
worry,
festering,
stifled,
self-persecution,
anger

Four Different Preservation Pressing Methods

Handle the herbs, leaves, and flowers with care; they are fragile and can tear easily. Using tweezers to transfer them is a good idea. Pressed specimen botanicals will fade naturally over time but keep them out of direct sunlight to delay fading. If you intend to glue your botanicals on to a paper or glass for example, use a clear, non-water-based variety. Otherwise, white craft glue or paper glue works fine. When preparing the flower for pressing, some thought should be given to how it will look when flattened. Avoid allowing parts to overlap. Leaves should normally be laid out flat.

Pressing Herbs, Leaves, and Flowers

- Gather clean specimens that are free of blemishes, spots, and bugs.
- Collect herbs and flowers on sunny mid-morning days when they are not too wet from rain or dew.
- Never gather species that are protected or endangered; if in doubt, check local regulations.
- Snip stems close to the base of the plant or leave them on if the stems are flat and thin.
- Find anything flat and heavy to act as a botanical press: a thick book, a heavy old chopping board, or a stone slab.
- If using a book to press your plants, protect the original book pages by placing the plants between two sheets of white paper before closing the book. Do not use paper towels as they may stick and/or leave an impression on your specimen. White inkjet computer paper is ideal. Should your specimen be bulky, add extra weight to the top of your press. A brick would be ideal.
- Now the hard part: Leave it undisturbed for a week to 10 days.
- At the end of a week to 10 days, open the book slowly. Now would be a good time to artfully paste and mount it or place it in a specimen envelope. Use tweezers to arrange and prevent damage should your specimen be thin and delicate.

For posterity, remember to identify the botanical specimen.

Name of Specimen: (common)_____ (scientific) _____

Date Gathered _____Location found _____

Name of Gather(s) _____

Microwaving

Some people like to shorten the drying period by using a microwave to dry the specimens. Put the entire book (with your specimen pressed between two white sheets of paper) into the microwave and zap in short bursts (15 seconds to a minute at a time, check frequently to see if they're done). Take great care not to over-cook your specimen. To finish its drying process, remove it from the microwave, let it cool, and then weigh the book down. Spot check it the next day. When it is completely dried, remove it with tender loving care. The drying process normally takes anywhere from a few hours to a day depending on the thickness of the specimen.

Ceramic Tile Microwave Press

Use two large ceramic tiles, two thick pieces of smooth cardboard (cut to the same size), and two pieces of white inkjet paper. Cardboard is highly absorbent and is an exceptionally good botanical blotter.

Layer your specimens as follows:

- Cardboard
- White inkjet paper
- Botanical specimen
- White inkjet paper
- Cardboard
- Ceramic tile

Cardboard Microwave Press

Eliminate the ceramic tile and simply use two thick pieces of smooth cardboard and two pieces of white inkjet paper then follow the layering instructions above.

Microwave pressing is not for everybody. Test the method using an ordinary leaf before trying it on your gathered specimens. For the serious specimen hunter and gatherer, there are specially made microwave presses that can be purchased. For more details, go to www.flower-press.com.

Traditional Wooden Press

A wooden press is often used for drying large groups of botanicals. If you are handy with a saw, here is a simple way to make one.

Supplies:
Buy a 1"x12" board that is three feet long, six long bolts (3-4 inches), and six wing nuts.

Instructions
Measure then cut the board in half. Drill six holes; one in each of the four corners and two holes one on each side centered midway between the corners of the board. Make sure the holes are big enough for the bolts to fit through and that the holes line up when you place one board on top of the other. This will allow you to bolt them together with the long bolts and wing nuts.

Layering and Pressing Specimens
Use two pieces of smooth, thick cardboard or newspaper between the boards for padding. Then layer as follows:

- Wood
- Cardboard blotter
- White ink jet paper
- Botanical specimen
- White ink jet paper
- Cardboard blotter
- Wood

Insert the long bolts into the holes and tighten the wing nuts down. If you are doing flowers, it would be a good idea to check and change the paper blotters at least every two days. The flowers will turn brown if they don't dry quickly.

Other Unique Pressing Methods
Some people prefer to use coffee filters as paper blotters for bulky flowers rather than inkjet paper.

In some cases, it helps to treat your plant materials with glycerin before pressing, especially with colorful leaves and flowers. Simply spray the glycerin on and allow the leaves or flowers to dry to the touch before pressing.

- Buy glycerin from a pharmacy or craft store and mix it with water. In a pinch, use fabric softener mixed with water.
- The mixture is 2 oz. of fabric softener or glycerin to a quart of water.

Wax paper and Ironing Press

Wax paper pressing is the quickest and the easiest method but is limited to flat botanicals like leaves, grass, and flower petals. The floral picture that opens this section is an example of this method.

Supplies
- Wax paper
- Ironing board and a warm iron
- Scissors
- Botanicals

Directions:
1. Cut two sheets of wax paper.
2. Place a sheet of wax paper on the ironing board.
3. Artfully arrange your botanicals on the wax paper.
4. Cover your chosen botanicals with a second sheet of wax paper.
5. Press down with a warm iron. Lift the iron every ten seconds. Press again repeating the process until the desired effect is accomplished. This seals the wax paper sheets together helping to preserve the botanicals at the same time. Word to the wise, do a test sample first.

Artistic Variations

Artfully trim the edges of the paper to give it a unique look. Add in confetti, glitter, sand, colorful feathers, stickers, pictures, etc. Liven up your project by using wood shavings, herbs, and spices. Add multicolor crayon shavings, acrylic paints, and perfume. Let your imagination enhance your project.

Pressing healing flowers, plants, and herbs is a tangible legacy that future generations will cherish and enjoy. While you are at it, create your own Moʻolelo, short stories, to further immortalize its worth. The survival of a culture depends on maintaining traditions. It's all up to you.

Lāʻau lapaʻau Practitioners in Hawaiʻi

The current status of Lāʻau lapaʻau being professionally practiced in Hawaiʻi is precarious at best.

Many have dabbled and studied the outer realms of this healing art and now profess to be experts. This sets a dangerous precedence for the legitimate practitioner because of opportunistic novices and charlatans hopping on the monetary "gravy train."

The Hawaiian culture contains a treasure throve of healing wealth that has been horribly exploited by the masses. The healing art of Lomi lomi massage is a definitive example of this travesty. While it is too late for Lomi lomi, it is with great hope that responsible Kumu Lāʻau lapaʻau, herbalists, will gather and unite to remedy this situation concerning Lāʻau lapaʻau.

Presently, there is an organization, Hui Mauli ola, that is attempting to stabilize this condition by setting agreed upon criteria to protect this healing art from being highjacked by the public at large. It is a daunting task as various Kumu Lāʻau lapaʻau experts "agree to disagree" on many of the healing protocols, practices, and remedies. This is always the case when it comes to native traditions as practices differ from island to island, district to district, family to family, and most importantly from Kumu to Kumu. Bear in mind these healing remedies evolved on remote islands; some were never shared, others reserved for family members, and still other remedies remain a protected secret.

Today's litigious society is the most valid reason why Kumu Lāʻau lapaʻau experts choose to remain anonymous. For those who wish to find a Kumu Lāʻau lapaʻau, contact the Office of Hawaiian Affairs (OHA).

The best recommendation this author can offer on finding a legitimate Kumu Lāʻau lapaʻau is to trust the "Coconut Wireless." Ask around. A word to the wise. Nāna i ke kumu, "look to the source", before ingesting herbal remedies.

Lāʻau lapaʻau Plant Sources in Hawaiʻi

For those in need of finding live or prepared native herbal plants, call any of the following contacts. Should they not have it, they will surely point you in the direction of someone who does.

ʻOahu

Foster Botanical Gardens	808 768-7135
Harold L. Lyon Arboretum	808 988-0456
Hoʻouluʻāina	808 841-7504
Hui kū maoli ola	808 295-7777
Native Ecosystem Services	808 469-9432
Native Plant Source	808 227-2019
Papa ola lōkahi	808 597-6651
UH Mānoa Campus Arboretum	808 956-8297

Maui

Hoʻolawa Farms	808 575-5099
Maui nui Botanical Gardens	808 249-2798
Native Nursery	808 936-2671

Hawaiʻi (Big Island)

Aikane Nursery	808 889-5906
Aileen's Nursery	808 936-2671
Amy B.H. Greenwell	808 323-3318
Big Island Plants (BIP)	808 985-8596

Lilikoi, Passionfruit, *Passiflora edulis*

Help Perpetuate Traditional Seeds of Truth
Kōkua e mau Moʻōlelo a ano o ʻoia
Kūkākūkā, Talk Story!

ʻAe	Yes
ʻAeʻa	Shiftless Wanderer
Ahi	Third Akua Spirit Sister
Ahuʻula	Feather Cape
ʻAi haʻa	Low Knee Bending Dance
ʻAina	Land
ʻAiwohikupua	Kauaʻi Chief, Sacred Child
Aka Cord	Soul Cord Spiritual Linkage
Akaka Falls	Waterfall
ʻĀkia	Toxic Shrub
Akua	Godly
ʻAlaʻalawainui	Hawaiian Mint, Poor Man's ʻAwa
ʻAlaea	Red Clay
ʻAliʻi	Royalty
Aliʻinui	Royal Chief
Aloha	Love
ʻAʻole	No
ʻAʻole mai	Don't Come Back
ʻApu	Cup
ʻAumakua	Ancestral Guardians
ʻAumakua Mauloa	Eternal Parent
ʻAwa	Bitter
ʻAwapuhi kuahiwi	Soap Ginger
Eʻepa	Abnormal
ʻEhu	Second Akua Spirit Sister
ʻEhu	Reddish Brown, Auburn
ʻEke	Bag

ʻEleʻele	Dark Black Eyes
ʻĒlemu	Buttocks
Hala	Offense
Hala Pūhala	Pandanus Tree, Screwpine
Hāloa	Progenitor
Hānāpepe	Island District on Kauaʻi
Hau	Hibiscus
Hauʻoki	Medicinal Tree Bark Akua
Hauʻoki	Male Akua Spirit Name
Hā	Breath
Haʻahaʻa	Humbleness
Hāʻupuʻupu	Hypnosis
Hele wale aku lā	Go into the Light
Hiʻaloa	Purgative
Hina	Female Demigod
Hina hina	Moss
Hiʻuwai	Water Purification Rite
Hoahānau	Cousin
Hōʻailona	Omen
Hoaloha	Friend
Hōkū	Star
Hōkūlaʻa ʻehu	Sacred Reddish Brown Stardust
Honomu	Island District on Big Island
Hoʻomālamalama	Enlightenment
Hoʻomalu ke keiki	Protect the Children
Hoʻopono pono	Conflict & Resolution

Hoʻokalakupua	Sorcery
Hoʻokalakupua ʻino	Black Magic
Houpo	Solar Plexus
Hūnā	Secret, Hidden
Hūnā Oli	Secret Entrapment Spell
Iʻaokepa	Cousin of Kaohu
Ihe,	Spear
ʻIliahi	Name of Masseuse
ʻIliahi	Sandalwood
ʻIke pāpā lua	Second-sight, Psychic, ESP
ʻIlima	Royal Flower
ʻIʻo	Soul Symbol, Hawk
ʻIwaʻiwa	Fern
ʻIno	Wicked, Bad, Malevolent
Ila	Birthmark
ʻIole	Rat
ʻIwaʻiwa	Maidenhair Fern
ʻIwaʻiwa	Name of Honomu Maidan
Kaea	Chieftess of Chief Luanuʻu
Kāʻekeʻeke	Bamboo Instrument
Kahakai	Maiden Lover of Kuahiwi
Kahiki	A Faraway Place
Kahuna Aloha	Love Master
Kahuna Aloha hui	Order of Love Masters
Kahuna Hāʻupuʻupu	Hypnotist, Autosuggestion

Kahuna Lāʻau lapaʻau	Master Herbalist
Kahuna Nui	Highest Ranking Priest
Kahuna Pule	Prayer Specialist
Kaimuki	Island District on Oāhu
Kake	Coded Language
Kākou	All of us
Kalo	Taro, Tubular Root
Kalaunuiohua	Big Island Chief
Kamakanuiahailono	First Lāʻau lapaʻau Herbalist
Kamaliʻi	Native Children
Kamapuaʻa	Boar Demigod
Kamehameha	The Great King
Kanaloa	Major Demigod (Female Aspect)
Kāne	Major Demigod
Kaohu	Cousin of Iʻaokepa
Kaomi lomilomi	Deep Tissue Massage
Kaona	Double meaning, Innuendos
Kapa	Cloth Blanket
Kapu	Restraints, Forbidden, Taboo
Kauaʻi	Oldest Hawaiian Island
Kaʻu	District on the Big Island
Kauwā	Outcast
Kava	Narcotic Brew
Ke aliʻi ʻai kanaka	Cannibal Chief
Kealiʻiwahilani	Name of a Princess

Kihei	Garment
Kī	Ti Leaf
Kilo ʻuhane	Mystic Spiritualist
Kīnehe	Name of Herbalist & Plant
Kinolau	Changeling, Shapeshifting, Body Forms
Koaliʻawa	Morning Glory
Kolohe	Naughty, Mischievous
Kapu	Restricted, Reserve, Forbidden
Kāula	Prophet
Keʻelikōlani	Princess Ruth
Keiki	Child
Kekuiapoiwa	Mother of King Kamehameha
Keoua	Chief of Kohala & Kona
Kï	Ti Leaf, Cordyline
Kïnehe	Spanish Needle
Kinolau	Supernatural Shapeshifting Body
Koʻolau	Oahu Mountain Range
Koʻokoʻolau Kīnehe	Ghost Needle, Biden Tea
Kōʻuahi a Pele	Red Sugarcane
Kū	Major Demigod
Kuʼi	Strike
Kuawa	Guava
Kuahiwi	Male Lover of Kahakai
Kuaʻiwa.	Young Chief
Kualiʻi	Name of Elderly Chief

Kūkaekōleapūʻoheʻohe	Job's Tears
Kūkeanēnē	Goose Dung Berries
Kūkona	Chief of Kauaʻi
Kukui	Candlenut
Kūkaniloko	Royal Birthing Refuge on Oahu
Kumu Hula	Dance Instructor
Kumuleilani	Name of a Princess
Kumu Pepei	Name of a Dance Instructor
Kuna	Shapeshifting Lizard Man
Kūkona	Island Chief of Kauaʻi
Kupua	Supernatural Shapeshifting Deity
Lāʻau	Plants
Lāʻau lapaʻau	Herbs
Lāʻau palau	War Club
Lāʻī	Ti leaf, Cordyline
Laʻi	Name of a Demigod
Laka	Forest Goddess and Dance
Laka	Goddess Namesake
Lani kuakaʻa	Highest Realm of Heaven
Laukahi	Plantain
Lauoho o Pele	Hair Strand of Pele
Lehuaokalani	Red Shark Goddess
Lumi uʻaʻa	Worthless Seaweed
Loli	Sea Slug, Sea Cucumber
Loli	Lusty Demigod Changeling

Lomilomi	Massage		Molemole	Bald
Lono	Major Demigod		Moloka'i	Island
Lono	Name of a Ka'u District Chief		Mo'olelo Pōkole	Short Stories
Lonopuha	First Lā'au lapa'au Chief		Mai'a	Banana
Luanu'u	High Chief		Mālama	To Care For, To Tend
Luika	Maiden Victim of Loli		Māmaki	Native Tea
Mahalo nui	Thank You Very Much		Makanikeoe	Name of Kahuna Aloha Master
Mahoe	Name of a Boy Twin		Māui	Demigod
Maika'i no	Wonderful, Great!		Maui	Hawaiian Island
Makanikeoe,	Master Kahuna Aloha		Mauli hā ola	Souls' Departing Breath
Maka'āinana	Commoner, Citizen, Populace		Mea'ai	Dessert
Makaloa	Third Eye		Melemele	Name of First Akua Spirit Sister
Makapu'u	Windward Beach on Oāhu		Mele	Maiden of the 'Ohe Grove
Makua	Parent		Mona	Name of a Girl Twin
Mala	Maiden of Waianae		Mo'o	Lizard
Mālama'ulu'okalani	Wife of Demigod Kū		Mo'opuna	Grandchild
Mana	Life Force Supernatural Energy		Nala	Weaving Technique
Mana'o	Thoughts, Input, Knowledge		Nalalaniapilihala,	Maiden of Pūhala Cave
Manawale'a	Generosity		Nāmaka o Hina	Noni Apple
Ma'o	Cotton		Nānā i ke kumu,	Look to the Source
Maoli	Hawaiian Native		Naupaka	Fan Flower
Manokalanipō	Original Name of Kaua'i		Na'au	Intestines
Manokalanipō	Heir of Chief Kūkona		Niaupi'o	Princess
Māunu	Molting, to Shed		Nīoi	Chile Pepper
Mea'ole	It's Nothing, You're Welcome		Niu	Coconut

Noho pū	Sitting Form of Meditation
Noni na maka o Hina	Polynesian Noni Apple
Nui Manu	Humanity
ʻOhe	Bamboo
ʻOhiʻaʻai	Mountain Apple
ʻOhe hano	Nose Flute
ʻOki	Cut, Sever
ʻŌlelo haʻi mua	Preface
ʻŌlena	Ginger Blossom or Root
Oli	Chant
Oʻopahu	Digging Stick
ʻŌpū	Belly intestines
Paeʻpae wāwae	Footstool
Paʻakai	Sea Salt
Pāʻakiki	Stubborn, Difficult
Pele	Fire Goddess
Peleuli	Native Queen
Pepeiao	Tree Ears, Wood Fungi
Piko Manawa	Fontanelle Crown Chakra
Pilikia	Trouble
Pilikino	Esoteric Body Blueprint
Pua Aliʻi	Royal Flowers (Children)
Puakala	Name of King's Handmaiden
Pale keiki	Midwife
Poi	Taro Root, Mush

Pohā	Gooseberry
Pōhaku	Stones
Poliʻahu	Snow Goddess
Pōpolo	Nightshade Berry
Puakala	Opioid flower
Pueo	Owl
Pūhala	Pandanus, Screwpine
Tī, Kī, Lāʻī	Cordyline
Tūtū	Grandparent
ʻUala	Sweet Potato
ʻUha loa, Hiʻaloa	Purgative noxious weed
Uhane makā ʻeo	Angry eye
ʻUlu	Breadfruit
ʻUlu	Child Heir of Kū
ʻUlu	Name of Midwife
Uwē	Alas
Wahiawa	District on Oāhu
Wai hoʻāno	Holy Water
Waianae	West Oahu District
Waiʻolani	Maiden of Molokaʻi
Waikanaloa	Name of a Wet Cave on Kauaʻi
Wākea	Mythical Ancestor Progenitor
Wehe ʻike Paipala	Bible Prophecy
Wohi akaʻaliʻi	Sacred Shadow King

Dr. Elithe Manuha'aipo Aguiar Kahn is a Kanaka maoli, an indigenous native of Hawai'i. She served as Kahu, Mentor of Mysticism, of Zen Care for 25 years, a healing center dedicated to traditional Hawaiian healing arts that focused on balancing the mental, physical, emotional, and spiritual human condition. She has authored several books on the subject: "HĀ Breathe!" *The Voice of the Shell Sounds, 'Ou Ka Leo O ka Pū,* "Ho'olei" *Activating Makaloa, "The Third Eye",* "MU" *Descendants - Origins of Hawaii Spirituality, Remnants of Mu,* "If Feet Could Talk" *Lomi Wāwae, The Healing Art of Hawaiian Foot Therapy,* "Legends of Hawai'i" *Lani Goose, Hawaiian Storyteller,* and "Aloha" *Folk Harp Music Book.* Dr .Kahn has also created the "Rainbow Blessings & Pearls of Wisdom", a self-help pictorial & guidebook system. Her passions are spiritual counseling, lunar astrology, research, writing, storytelling, gardening, composing music, and playing the harp. She is a resident harpist at Nu'uanu Hale, a long-term care center. Currently, she is working on a Hawaiian astrological and lunar forecasting system. When she is not traveling abroad, she counsels at Hawai'i Pacific Healing Center in Honolulu, Hawai'i.

Credentials

Doctor of Philosophy in Metaphysics, *American Institute of Holistic Theology*
Master of Science in Metaphysics
BA Psychology, *Hawai'i Pacific University*
AA Liberal Arts, *University of Hawai'i*
Hypnotherapist, *Omni Hypnosis Training Center*
Hawaiian Storyteller (*Lani Goose*) *Mo'olelo Pōkole*
Lunar Astrologist *Hōlani*

CPSIA information can be obtained
at www.ICGtesting.com
Printed in the USA
LVHW050730050822
725199LV00003B/113